Christ—
The Original Matrix

Christ—
The Original Matrix

God Face-to-Face

TIMOTHY D. CARROLL

foreword by Richard K. Murray

RESOURCE *Publications* · Eugene, Oregon

CHRIST—THE ORIGINAL MATRIX
God Face-to-Face

Resource Publications
An Imprint of Wipf and Stock Publishers
199 W. 8th Ave., Suite 3
Eugene, OR 97401

www.wipfandstock.com

PAPERBACK ISBN: 978-1-7252-7827-1
HARDCOVER ISBN: 978-1-7252-7828-8
EBOOK ISBN: 978-1-7252-7829-5

Manufactured in the U.S.A.   09/30/20

Contents

Foreword

TIM CARROLL'S SUBTITLE SAYS it all, "*God face-to-face.*" This book provides an organic overview of how and why we should treasure interfacing with God. No easy task, yet God is unveiled here by Tim's prismatic prose as attractive, approachable, accessible, and awe-inspiring.

As I read Tim's book, I couldn't help but draw comparisons to Martin Buber's 20th century classic, *I and Thou*, the perfect primer on the relational dynamics between God and man. The obvious difference is that Buber wrote from the Hebraic perspective, while Tim writes from the Christian viewpoint. Yet both tenderly resonate with one another. They each reveal a God who, above all else, inhabits and prioritizes the realm of ongoing relationship.

God is first revealed as the motherly "womb" (matrix) of all our beings which continues to develop us, then as the universal "Father of lights" who is the gallant guardian of all our souls, and finally, as the Logos-infused incarnation of Jesus who, as the first born of many brethren, leads us all into direct and unmediated intimacy with God. The question then becomes *not* "What about God *is* relational?"—*but* instead— "What about God *isn't* relational?"

After first presenting us a conceptual canvass illustrating the rainbow hues of relationship between God and humanity, Tim then develops a messianic metaphysic through which we can discover our own cosmic origin along with our transcendent destiny. He takes us on this journey with the church fathers, George MacDonald, C.S. Lewis, Hans von Balthasar, and others to help us seize the epiphany that we all are sparked with divinity.

And these living sparks want to set our lives and world ablaze with the curative energies of God.

As Tim sagely notes, we were created *in* God's image, and *with* God's substance. It doesn't get any better than that. As described by Tim, God's divine alchemy in blending and forming us into His image-bearers is both jaw dropping and breath taking.

This incredible treasure may be imbedded in earthen vessels, but "under the arctic ice," as Tim notes, there is a depth of divinity waiting to be unveiled, unfurled, and unionized with other believers.

Here is Tim's magnificent point: all of humanity has an individual and corporate date with destiny. Our individual destiny, as a child of God, and our corporate destiny, as the fully formed bride of Christ, will all experientially converge so that "Christ will be all in all." The ice will melt, our hearts will melt, and all creation will melt and meld into the humanity and divinity of Christ. Now *that's* divine alchemy.

P.S. Tim's final chapter is worth the price of admission alone. In it, he presents his Ninety—Five Theses defending the reconciliation of all things in Christ. Each of these nuggets is spiritual gold. They cumulatively provide irresistible wisdom from Scripture that Jesus is indeed Salvador Mundi, the Savior of the World.

RICHARD K. MURRAY

Prologue

THIS BOOK IS HOPEFULLY the first of a trilogy. In writing this book, it is a fulfillment of something I have desired for a long time. Yet, I am happy I did not write it until recently as I have altered some of my views in the past few years. Although the task of writing this has been near three years in duration, it has really been something I've been writing my entire life. Yet, it is not about me, but rather about anybody and everybody.

Some insight into the unfolding of the contents of this little book. It started with the divine Logos and thoughts concerning creation. In fact, that was initially my first chapter. It is in this chapter where I deal with the subject of *God face-to-face*.

While writing this book, I had gained two significant insights that I had not previously considered. First, when contemplating about *In His Image*, I had drawn some conclusions that were entirely new to me. I consider it an epiphany and I have no regrets in sharing those thoughts with the reader. Second, I accidently stumbled across certain terms and found myself using phrases that I would have one time considered New Age.

I struggled in English from grade school through college, even requiring a tutor to help me get a passing grade. I recall my first day of grade school, my parents lived close enough that I was able to walk there (Ross Elementary—Sweet Valley, Pennsylvania). At lunch time, my mother said that she turned around in the kitchen and there I was. She asked why I was home? I had replied, "Me tried it, me no like it, me quit!"

I must acknowledge a few people for a moment. I am a blessed man with a wonderful wife and family, of which this book would not have come to pass without them. I am grateful for all the encouragement and support.

To my wife Debbie, daughter Nicole, son Austin and stepson Matthew, here it is—the book is finally completed! The assistance and 'first round' corrections and constructive feedback from Debbie, Nicole and Austin was helpful.

A very warm thanks is also due to friend Dave Waggoner for sparing the time necessary to perform the final editing of the manuscript, coupled with suggestions to improve the reading of this book.

I am also appreciative of the support of Sunshine Cathedral Church (Plant City, Florida), where I shared the contents of this book, allowing me to flush out ideas. Likewise, a special heartfelt thank you to John and Joan Tabone (Pittston, Pennsylvania), who helped a young man some thirty-seven years ago. You both were there for me when I needed it the most.

In closing, if you were to ask me, what is one thing that I hope people will say about this book, my prayer is that this book aides the reader to an inward vision, to discover that great mystery of Christ in you, the hope of glory.

Blessings

TDC

1

The Idea of Matrix

CALL ME THEOPHILUS. We are immensely loved by God. Whether we know it or not, there is absolutely nothing that can separate us from his constant love towards us. We are to understand that we are his most excellent Theophilus.

Have you ever noticed that the apostle Luke used the name of "Theophilus" when addressing the audience of his only known two letters? He wrote, "It seemed good to me also, having perfect understanding of all things from the very first, to write unto thee in order, most excellent Theophilus" (Luke 1:3). And again, "The former treatise have I made, O Theophilus, of all that Jesus began both to do and teach" (Acts 1:1).

This salutation was an expression of endearment. It means beloved of God, loved of God, friend of God or lover of God. Some may think that Luke was addressing a specific person about whom there are many conjectures and traditions around the supposed identity of such a person. It seems far more reasonable that Luke was addressing the beloved in Christ.

In fact, hear the words of Origen Adamantius of Alexandria (AD 185—253), who is universally recognized as one of the greatest religious thinkers and theologians of the Christian Church. He states, "Anyone who is Theophilus is both excellent and very strong; this is what the Greek word (excellent) actually means. No Theophilus is weak. Scripture says of the people of Israel, when they were going out of Egypt, 'there was no weakling in their tribes.' I could say that everyone that is a Theophilus is robust. He has vigor and strength both from God and his Word. He can recognize the truth of those words, by which he has been instructed and understand the Word of the Gospel in Christ . . ."[1]

In the great classical book, *Moby Dick*, the author Herman Melville opened with the words, CALL ME ISHMAEL. I did not have much success in reading his entire book, albeit one day I may. But permit me to ask you, dear reader, this question: So, how do you view or consider your own self? Better yet, what would you have others say of you as a person?

A long time ago, I had boasted of being a self-pronounced atheist. I lacked the belief in the existence of God. Perhaps deep down I did believe he existed but simply didn't care about me nor anyone else for that matter. Maybe the notion of God did not completely escape me, after all, I did attend church from time-to-time with my parents as a youngster.

So, perhaps I was more of an agnostic, not believing God could be known or understood. Regardless, it simply did not matter to me in the least, especially when attending college. As an unbeliever at the time, I find it odd that there were times I had certain thoughts toward him, even to the extent of making requests and promises to him in my mind. Then at other moments, I had found I would be better served to have my final place in hell. I can't say whether I had thought this honestly or hypocritically. Perhaps I was expecting some sort of favor or mercy in consequence of the confession?

Most of all, I vividly recall another evening while hanging out with some college friends, I had publicly denounced God in utter contempt and disdain, challenging him, if he existed that is! Indeed, CALL ME ISHMAEL at the time.

Yet, only a few months later after graduation, I, who supposedly did not believe in God, found myself in anguish and despair, overwhelmed with numerous disappointments all hitting me at once. And there I found myself, having forty-plus sleeping pills lodged in my stomach, with my ears ringing, hoping to die. Then suddenly, I began crying out to Jesus to help me, begging for his assistance! Numerous times from my lips were the words, "Jesus, Jesus, please help me." I can still recall that very dark moment as if it were yesterday. I spent the weekend in the hospital recovering. Two years later, I had made another attempt. I have not shared these incidents with many people, perhaps out of shame and embarrassment. And now, my loved ones know.

---

1. Origen, *Homiles on Luke*, 9

Perhaps another reason for my silence: There are some Christians who thrive on the dramatic conversion story, whereas I have a slightly different perspective. I have always given thought to Paul's testimony that he counted all things but dung that he may win Christ. Therefore, it is my tendency to avoid too much emphasis and chit-chat about former mistakes and fleshly engagements of futility. Yet, it would be quite accurate to say, I had needed someone to rescue me from my downward spiral and to deliver me from my own destruction and lower-base self.

Now more than thirty-seven years have since come and gone and I can now say in all humility and gratitude, with the utmost confidence, I am not to be called an atheist nor Ishmael, of that I am certain. Rather, in my spirit, I can hear the words, CALL ME THEOPHILUS, call me the object of his love, the loved of God, a lover of God!

So, do we know who we are, where we came from, and to whom we return? The apostle Paul said it this way, "For of him, and through him, and to him, are all things: to whom be glory forever. Amen" (Rom 11:36). To consider that there could be a divine Being behind the creation of humanity, a God if you will, can be staggering to the mind. Certainly, some may contend such a notion to be presumptuous as I had thought once myself, but that is not our subject at this moment. Rather, I am convicted of my overwhelming experience and sense of belonging to something greater, belonging to the source of all things. And if I belong, I dare say, I must have something in common.

I know we have all had such a yearning or craving one time or another, something within desiring to be liberated, to have dignity and value, in search of something, to be connected and restored to a place of meaning, of purpose and destiny, desiring something higher than our current condition of soul-life. It is as the Psalmist stated, "Deep calleth unto deep" (Ps. 42:7), having that which is common, as Deep calls unto its own.

Humanity is not conscious of its own origin or identity. We have something in common from whence we came as well as with one another. The relationship is there whether we realize it or not. Our own experience has proven that we all are in some way connected with one another, not separate and uncommon. That which connects us can only come from God himself, and from which humanity originated.

No person truly lives unto themself when you think about it. We are eventually all connected in some way, all related. As it has been said by many others, when one suffers, they do not suffer alone, and when one lives a rich and vibrant life, another is the beneficiary. The apostle Paul even said when one member suffers, all suffer with it, and if one be honored, all rejoice.

Most certainly bonded, and I dare say, that meaningful connection can only be found in the Christ of God.

When I consider something having a myriad of connections, I think of a matrix. Yet not in the abstract, but rather relating with one another in some way, perhaps even personal. Furthermore, I find it most interesting that the Merriam Webster Dictionary defines a "matrix" as something within or from which something originates or develops. This idea far exceeds some sort of force or energy. This must be dynamic, personally intimate, and even life–giving. This can only be a divine being or deity which can integrate all the components of life and demonstrate the essential connection points and relationships between himself, humanity, and all of creation. This original matrix can be none other than the Christ of God.

When we find ourselves lost in our separateness from this matrix of life and personal being, which is the Christ, we become detached from our commonality. Yet, we must come to understand that our belonging far exceeds the notion that God was only our creator. Birds, bees, flowers, and trees have that much in common.

I think it is fair to say when considering this great matrix of humanity, when each person comes into his rightful place, we all will have discovered, though we may have once been separated in the darkness of our mind, we were never detached in our spirit from God. He has been closer than we have ever imagined. He has always been there from the very start. Every thought, before it came to mind, he knew it because he was there. When you dismissed him and even separated yourself in thought, he could not abandon you, for he can't deny himself. My friend, when we grasp that humanity and divinity are inseparable, that humanity is part of the life of God, we will discover, as did Jacob, that God was in this place and we knew it not (Gen 28:16).

The very notion of eternity is beyond our comprehension, yet we strive to understand, to grasp the unknown. The concept of 'beyond yonder' can be perplexing at times. We look up into the sky and it never ends. We gaze into the physical expression of infinity. Where does it start, where does it end, as if thinking the earth were flat and simply falls off? I think existence continues into infinity itself, which has no end; it simply goes on and on. The universe in which we live is not some sort of illusion. It is a matrix of ideas, which are an expression of an infinite God, a source of life which sustains and holds all things together.

The idea of "God" carries myriads of thoughts bombarding our minds. When the true and living God is revealed to the human mind, it is a beautiful moment and experience. Yet, we must come to realize that such a God, in all his diversity, is still unity, is still harmony and is most definitely One.

It should come as no surprise that we get our single word "universe" from compacting together the words unity and diversity. Is it not the same with God and his connections? The one and yet the many, the connectedness of the matrix, all aiming for the highest good of humanity.

We find ourselves reaching through from what "is seen" to the reality beyond. I ask, where is this so–called beyond? I think it can be better asked, where is it not? "If I ascend into heaven, thou art there: if I make my bed in hell, behold, thou art there" (Ps 139:8). How can there be anything in the universe outside of God? Yet, we so often think of God as outside and reaching down to us. He keeps it all connected and he is so incredibly close. So close, that it becomes every bit uniquely personal. Oh, if the truth can only be told, he resides deep within the soul of every person. This is the mystery of Christ within you.

The early twentieth–century Anglican theologian and Oxford scholar, R.J. Campbell, put it quite well by saying, "It is that in every man there is a latent Christ. The touch of the Divine Spirit wakens that Christ within and brings Him into union with the Christ above. As Origen so sweetly put it centuries ago, 'Christ sleeps in the soul of every man as he slept in the boat on the Lake of Galilee, and he wakes at the cry of penitence to still the storm of sinful passion in our lives.'"[2]

Amen! The latent Christ in every person and, at the appropriate time, he awakens and becomes your very salvation. A long time ago, when he first revealed himself to me, I was reading and thought, "how can it say that every eye shall see him?" It then dawned upon me that it was the inner eye of the spirit within man that shall see him. Our very own being is derived from the source of life, from the very God that created man. Remove God from our being and you forfeit the entire human race. We may not comprehend nor be aware of it, but the apostle Paul addressed the very same question, as it had been always at the forefront in the minds of ancient thinkers. Answering the three great mysteries of life, motion, and being, when Paul spoke on Mars Hill to the men of Athens of the unknown God, he said, "For in him we live, and move, and have our being" (Acts 17:28). It is important we understand that this is something that is not eventually or ultimately true but rather immediately true.

I think of the ancient thinkers or philosophers who had given themselves to the contemplation of such things. In Philosophy, there was Thales, who was considered the father of Western Greek thought. He examined the idea of life and creation's need of water. He also contributed thoughts toward the idea of motion and solved a problem of diverting the flow of

2. Campbell, *The Song of Ages*, 152

a river. He was on a quest for discovering ultimate reality. Then there was Heraclitus who thought of all things flowing and in a state of becoming. For him, whatever *is* was always changing and he referenced fire always transforming. Then there was Parmenides who supposedly asserted "whatever *is*, is." His contemplation of being was not one that was becoming but one that simply is. For him, for something to exist, it must be. So, two great minds, one was focused on "becoming" and the other on "being."

Though there were others, none really matched the three titans of philosophical thought: Socrates, Plato and Aristotle. Socrates stated that an "unexamined life is not worth living." He awakened others to a deeper sense of truth, both in terms of how we think and how we live. His goal was to educate people out of their ignorance and come to an understanding of virtue. Then his student, Plato, was both an idealist and realist, indicating that the meaning of ultimate reality is based on a theory of ideas. His approach seemed to resolve the tension between the two prior thoughts of Parmenides and Heraclitus, the becoming and the being, the flux and permanence, the change and non–change. Then came Plato's student, Aristotle, known as "the philosopher," and teacher to Alexander the Great. It is said that his understanding of God influenced the much later thinking of Thomas Aquinas.

I am suspended in awe when contemplating Christ, the One that resides within us. I am overwhelmed with the myriad of dependencies and connections, each building on the other when I consider this new man as it relates to the twelve sayings of Jesus, specifically marked by reiterated amen(s) in the writings of the apostle of love, John. All connected in perfect harmony, as in a divine matrix.

My friend, there is no escaping the undeniable fact that it is impossible to be outside of God. We never were and never can be. The reality is that we are connected to him in terms of our true being because we came from him. Our minds need to be reconciled to that fact. To be entirely forthright, whether you profess to be a Christian or not, every person ought to know that each is a part of the totality of the divine Being. I just so happen to believe that certain parts of Christianity and various church fathers had gotten it more accurate than other religions, coming to the revelation and discovering that the Christ is none other than the divine Logos from ancient times, of which our Lord Jesus Christ is the full revelation and perfect manifestation.

If we all belong to God, if by some means we are joined by an invisible and spiritual bond, then it would also suggest we are connected in humanity, related in a way that is beyond any physical existence. The totality of human beings includes those in the afterlife. Only in this divine matrix, the

Christ of God, will we begin to find our linkage with our fellow man. Only then will we discover the reality of our own being, and the immediate connection with other beings. You, my dear Theophilus, serve as a critical link in that very chain of being.

2

The Fatherhood of God

WE MUST COME TO know that God is the father of all of humanity and the very source of being. It could be said this way, "God is our father. He has always been our father. There has never been a time when God was not our father. We haven't always known this. But now we do."

Let us not make the mistake to think that all of humanity are not his children. Those that make such a distinction of "us" and "them" can fall into all sorts of attitudes of exclusivity and even divine nationalism and separation, as did the Jews. It may also skew how we look upon others, having the unspoken and deeply hidden "my–father–only" syndrome, thinking we are preferred more than others in some odd way. Permit me to clear up the misconception that some may have on the very subject of universal fatherhood.

First and foremost, Luke indicates that Adam was the son of God (Luke 3:38). The words "*son of*" are in italics in the King James version of the Bible and are not in the original Greek. In fact, the genealogy of Christ in this chapter begins with Joseph, his stepfather. Yet, it can't be dismissed that it depicts a linkage to the one that had provided fatherly guidance, in most cases, their natural father. Furthermore, it should be clear to anyone that God gendered Adam, thereby making God his father. To deny this fact is utter foolishness and nonsense.

We find Paul saying, "For though there be that are called gods, whether in heaven or earth . . . But to us one God, the Father, of whom are all things, and we in him; and one Lord Jesus Christ, by whom are all things, and we by him" (1 Cor 8:5–6). Again, he said, "There is . . . One God and Father of all, who is above all, and through all, and in you all" (Eph 4:6). Take notice to what Paul said, there is one God, the Father, of whom are all things. He also said, One Father of all. Likewise, Paul understood the Hebrew Scriptures quite well, such as ". . .the God of the spirits of all flesh" (Num 16:22). We find the writer of Hebrews referring to the same when he said ". . . shall we not much rather be in subjection unto the Father of spirits, and live" (Heb 12:9)?

One of my favorite stories in scripture is of two sons and the love of their father. I am sure you know of it, as it is quite popular among Christian churches, whether Orthodox, Catholic or Protestant. It is known as the parable of the prodigal son and the common emphasis is about one son that had gone astray. Yet, it is the story of two sons and the love of one father. In fact, there are many narratives or story lines, a few of which we shall explore herein.

First you should know, it is a parable given by Jesus himself. He continually spoke in parables, especially when it was regarding the kingdom of God. A parable is an analogy, a representation or analogous story, a simile or picture–story. It is used to illustrate essential points of truth. The parable is not the truth within itself but a story to lead its hearer to the reality of the matter.

In fact, we find this story of the lost prodigal as one of five stories (lost sheep, lost coin, prodigal son, the unjust steward, and the rich man and Lazarus) in a single parable in the gospel of Luke as he spoke *the* parable (Luke 15:3), albeit the entire parable is not the subject of our topic at this moment. Though a convincing case can be made to explain how Jesus masterfully used five stories in parabolic form to describe the self–righteous Pharisees and scribes in comparison to publicans and sinners, I shall use this one story to illustrate a few points worthy of our consideration.

This story is really about the love of a father towards two sons and though I will mostly focus on the one that lost his way, permit me to touch briefly on the other son as well. Although it is a direct story about the Jews and Gentiles of that day, it speaks to all of us to some degree.

The story reads as follows, Luke writes of Jesus saying, "A certain man had two sons: And the younger of them said to his father: Father, give me the portion of goods that falleth to me. And he divided unto him his living. And not many days after the younger son gathered all together, and took his journey into a far country, and there wasted his substance with riotous living. And when he had spent all, there arose a mighty famine in the land;

and he began to be in want. And he went and joined himself to a citizen of that country; and he sent him into his fields to feed swine. And he would have fain filled his belly with the husks that the swine did eat; and no man gave unto him.

"And when he came to himself, he said, how many hired servants of my fathers have bread enough and to spare, and I perish with hunger! I will arise and go to my father, and will say unto him, Father I have sinned against heaven, and before thee, and am no more worthy to be called thy son: make me as one of thy hired servants. And he arose and came to his father. But when he was yet a great way off, his father saw him, and had compassion, and ran, and fell on his neck, and kissed him. And the son said unto him, Father, I have sinned against heaven, and in thy sight, and am no more worthy to be called thy son. But the father said to his servants, Bring forth the best robe, and put it on him; and put a ring on his hand, and shoes on his feet: And bring hither the fatted calf, and kill it; and let us eat, and be merry. For my son was dead, and is alive again; he was lost, and is found. And they began to be merry . . ." (Luke 15:11–24).

The first point to bring to your attention is to notice the disposition of the father towards the lost son. He did not say, "you have embarrassed our name and family, you ought to be ashamed of your riotous living with harlots and spending your inheritance wildly and foolishly." No, but rather the father saw his son from a distance and ran to him with open arms, having not contempt but compassion towards him; waiting patiently for him, and then embracing him, ready to place the best robe, ring and shoes on him, and to have a feast with the celebration of music and dancing. What a beautiful story of a loving and compassionate father and his alienated son. The reconciliation is effectual immediately upon his return. He may have been a lost son, yet still very much and always a son as far as the father was concerned.

We all understand this father to be God and most of us seem to gravitate towards this story by identifying with it in some degree, whether our sin is great or small, nevertheless, we most always consider ourselves to be the lost son in some way, shape or form. The story states the son came to himself, realizing his folly. Yes, the father left him to the consequences of his own sins, permitted him to go, to learn of the husks and swine. His journey ought not to be applauded as the way of the transgressor is difficult and what a man sows, he reaps. However, the story teaches us of God's mercy towards us in the worst of situations, and his very thoughts toward us can be no different than in this story of the prodigal son, as spoken by Jesus Christ.

I often wondered, what if the younger son did not return? Would the father have turned bitter and vindictive towards him? Would his love have eventually waxed cold with hatred and punitive vengeance? Clearly Jesus was teaching us that the father is no such person. Such is a loving father in the parable; such is a loving father in heaven towards his lost creation! This story provides incredible insight into the heart of God towards those who are lost in their ways, as God–the–Father waits patiently without contempt, hostility, anger, vengeance or wrath; waiting in mercy, compassion, loving–warmth and open arms to receive them.

Luke continued to tell of Jesus saying, "Now his elder son was in the field: and as he came and drew nigh to the house, he heard music and dancing. And he called one of the servants and asked what these things meant. And he said unto him, Thy brother is come: and thy father hath killed the fatted calf, because he hath received him safe and sound. And he was angry, and would not go in: therefore came his father out, and intreated him.

"And he answering said to his father, Lo, these many years do I serve thee, neither transgressed I at any time thy commandment: and yet thou never gavest me a kid, that I might make merry with my friends: But as soon as this thy son was come, which hath devoured thy living with harlots, thou hast killed for him the fatted calf. And he said unto him, Son, thou art ever with me, and all that I have is thine. It was meet that we should make merry and be glad: for this thy brother was dead, and is alive again; and was lost, and is found" (Luke 15: 25–32).

Secondly, there are some reading this now who may have never really been as a prodigal son but rather more like the elder son in the story. Oh, I am not suggesting that you have been sinless or without flaw, but all and in all, you have never allowed your soul to drift too far away, always maintaining your sense of your heavenly father. Perhaps to some degree, Luke was realizing his own life as well, not left afar to riotous living, but rather serving his fellowman as a physician. So, the older brother was upset, that is understandable. Yet, after he complains of never having been given a celebration with his friends, what do we read of his father? Did the father respond in a spiteful or harsh tone and reprove him? No, his father told him, "thou art ever with me, and all that I have is thine. It was meet that we should make merry and be glad: for this thy brother was dead, and is alive again; and was lost, and is found" (Luke 15:31–32).

Jesus stops the story here and does not tell whether the older son goes into the celebration or not. Far be it from us to assume the older son did not go into the celebration with his father. This again tells of the love that the father had for the elder son. Many have misunderstood this son too, assuming Jesus was teaching that the Pharisees were nothing but self–righteous and undeserving. It is obvious that the appeal was to see what his Pharisee listeners might do, including them to join in the celebration.

Thirdly, parts of religion have used this story to illustrate the so-called depravity of human nature. Needless-to-say, man is certainly capable of his wayward digression and a downward spiral only to be found in a far-away place from his heavenly father and lost in his condition. But what says Jesus of the younger son in the story? Have you ever read his words without trying to fit, mold and twist them into a presumed system of religious thought? Jesus precisely said, "And when he came to himself. . . I will arise and go to my father." I dare say, this verse alone will bother plenty of my fellow brethren. Obviously, Jesus knew of something more noble in man. The prodigal came to "himself," to the higher side of his self rather than the lower-based self. He came to the divine side of himself which cannot be satisfied with the lowly living among the swine. This deeper discovery through his humiliation and suffering brings the realization of his belonging to his father, because his spiritual-being and nature could do no other.

As wonderful as this entire story is, one would miss out if not discovering how this is connected to other ideas from the stories within this entire single parable. As within a matrix, observe the additional connection points to better understand and relate to the whole. In the beginning of this same parable is another story, the sheep that was lost. It was not to be found with the ninety-nine at home but rather the one who had strayed away. In fact, it needed to be laid on the shoulders of the shepherd and carried back home. The sheep would know the voice of his shepherd and though lost, it did not resist being brought back to its rightful place.

Without this additional insight, we would all agree that the lost prodigal had returned to the place of his father to enjoy the benefits in which he had always been entitled, entirely on his own. However, we now see that it was the Christ in him that was in the far-away place, bringing him home. He came into contact, with the Christ as the Good Shepherd, to bring him to where he always belonged. He required intervention of the divine Christ within himself. He was once lost but now reconciled, thereby returning to the fold.

The father seeing his lost son is something far better than what religion has supposed of humanity. Not seen as a poor, totally depraved, unworthy, underserving, sinner barely saved by grace but rather considering him as something far greater—his own son whom he loved! Think of it.

But some object to the idea of universal fatherhood, some may ask, what about when Jesus said, "ye are of your father, the devil?" Let's first review the story, as it follows. "Then said Jesus to those Jews which believed on him, if ye continue in my word, then are ye my disciples, indeed; And ye shall know the truth, and the truth shall make you free. They answered him, we be Abraham's seed, and were never in bondage to any man: how sayest thou, Ye shall be made free? Jesus answered them, Verily, verily I say unto you, whosoever committeth sin is the servant of sin. And the servant abideth not in the house for ever, but the Son abideth ever. If the Son therefore shall make you free, ye shall be free indeed. I know that ye are Abraham's seed; but ye seek to kill me, because my word hath no place in you. I speak that which I have seen of my Father; and ye do that which ye have seen with your father.

"They answered and said unto him, Abraham is our father. Jesus saith unto them, if ye were Abraham's children, ye would do the works of Abraham. But now ye seek to kill me, a man that hath told you the truth, which I have heard of God; this did not Abraham. Ye do the deeds of your father. They said to him, we be not born of fornication; we have one Father, even God. Jesus said unto them, If God were your Father, ye would love me: for I proceeded forth and come from God; neither came I of myself, but he sent me. Why do ye not understand my speech? Even because ye cannot hear my word. Ye are of your father the devil, and the lusts of your father ye will do. He was a murderer from the beginning, and abode not in the truth, because there is no truth in him. When he speaketh a lie, he speaketh of his own, for he is a liar, and the father of it. And because I tell you the truth, ye believe me not . . ." (John 8:30–47).

At first glance it appears as if Jesus was denying that God was their father and rather confirming that the devil was their father, but he was not saying that in the least bit. If you read the context of the story closely, he is rather speaking of their likeness in character or their moral resemblance, not their origin of nature.

First notice the comparisons he makes with statements like: "I tell you the truth and ye believe me not" with "the devil is a liar"; or "ye seek to kill me" and "the devil was a murderer." Therefore, what does this say about them? Clearly, they were by resemblance the children of the devil and could not make the claim of God as their Father. Secondly, he likewise makes the comparison of "if ye were Abraham's children, ye would do the works of Abraham" and "if God were your Father ye would love me."

However, here is the point that is often missed or overlooked. They were very much the children of Abraham by descent. Their heritage and nature is something that Jesus never disputed or denied. However, they were in disbelief and their conduct did not resemble Abraham, who was urged on by faith to follow God. In fact, take careful notice that Jesus confirms they are of Abraham when he said, "I know that ye are Abraham's seed." Likewise, though they belonged to God as his children, they did not resemble him in their conduct.

So, Christ denies them both of Abraham and God as their Father, in context of resemblance of character. But he never denies them of it in terms of their seed and identity. To suggest otherwise is to miss the idea entirely and insert meaning contrary to what Christ clearly stated in the story.

Again, it was Jesus himself that said, "If ye then, being evil, know how to give good gifts unto your children, how much more shall your Father which is in heaven give good things to them that ask him" (Matt 7:11)? Jesus emphatically informed those being evil that God is their father.

Therefore, have we not all one father? Ask the prophet Malachi, as we find his words, "Have we not all one father? Hath not one God created us" (Mal 2:10)?

The idea of the Fatherhood of God was understood and not entirely foreign before Jesus preached it. The concept of God's goodness, kindness, compassion, and paternal love were already understood in ancient times, prior to the incarnation of Jesus Christ. To object is to deny history as well as human consciousness. And yet, Jesus Christ reminded his listeners and made the connection of God to Fatherhood, teaching and demonstrating to them the ideas of the compassion, forgiveness, and love.

3

The Divine Logos

By the revelation of God, Moses gave us the story of Genesis. We read his opening statements, "In the beginning God created the heaven and the earth. And the earth was without form, and void; and darkness was upon the face of the deep. And the Spirit of God moved upon the face of the waters. And God said, Let there be light: and there was light. And God saw the light, that it was good: and God divided the light from the darkness. And God called the light Day, and the darkness he called Night. And the evening and the morning were the first day" (Gen 1:1–5).

Who could ever express in an adequate manner the ideas of God regarding the creation of the world? Yet the exceeding beauty of the description of creation and a glimpse into how it unfolded is provided to us in Genesis. And at such time, who better than Moses should have provided this, a man who likely reached the very summit of his own contemplation of the Lord as well as being learned in all the wisdom of the Egyptians and surrounding nations. So, God illuminated the mind of Moses, and in turn he provided the story of creation to us. Yet one can hardly imagine that Moses came to such an understanding with no prior knowledge of the creation account to declare except that which he only obtained direct from God. In fact, ancient creation stories were part of other religions far before the Hebrew people adopted their own version.

I have come to understand, and have no reason to doubt, that the original text was more like, "In the beginning God created the heavens (plural) and the earth." This is not an analysis on original text meaning, albeit that would serve us well to a certain degree, but rather as the James Moffatt translation states, "This is the story of how the universe was formed," in which I say a hearty amen.

In reading the opening text and contemplating the original account of creation, we find that in the beginning (some may dispute it as 'in a beginning') God himself does something—he creates! Farrar Fenton, in his translation of the Bible renders the passage "By periods God created," or "beginnings." This first proclamation or insertion in scripture that God creates can be controversial as it sets our Christian faith apart from other competing "isms" and philosophies and religions for our allegiance and loyalty. We learn that he created, and he did it in the beginning. I am sure most understand this to mean starting point, the origin or genesis of something, in which I concur. But is this only about the beginning of something, namely time? You know, as stories often begin "once upon a time." Is it possible that this could mean much more? Certainly, it is not the origin of God for he cannot have a beginning, else we would have to then ask what was before that and what had caused it?

I find an interesting statement by the early Jewish historian Philo of Alexandria (a Mediterranean port city in Egypt with once a large Jewish population) who lived from about 20 BC to 50 AD.

He aptly stated, "for since time is the interval of motion of the heavens, there could not have been any such thing as motion before there was anything which could be moved."[1]

I must therefore ask the question—yet what more could this "beginning" have been in the opening three words of Genesis than the origin of time? Perhaps it is not a question of 'when'. To ask 'where' is to understand that it was *in* the beginning. I think John the beloved provides us with some further insight regarding this matter as his gospel opens with the phrase "In the beginning was the Word (Logos)." Now I do not think that he was saying "way back yonder was the Word," although that would certainly be a true statement. He said the beginning was the Word. We are to understand that the Word is the Logos, the divine logic, or idea and reasoning of God. In other words, it could be understood this way, "In the divine logic (beginning, Word) God created."

Now consider the words of John the revelator, "these things saith the Amen, the faithful and true witness, the beginning of the creation of God"

---

1. Yonge, *The Works of Philo*, 5

(Rev 3:14). What does he say about the beginning? He tells us that the beginning was the Amen, the faithful and a true witness. We can say that the Word or divine Logos was the same. The Word was the Amen, the faithful and true witness. The Word was the truth as Amen means truth or so be it. In fact, Isaiah said "God of truth" (Isa 65:16), or in the Hebrew "God Amen."

It is here in this beginning or Word where we also find many other things. Scripture tells us in the beginning is wisdom, knowledge, his kingdom, and strength. Indeed, the Word is wisdom; it is also an intimate knowing and experience (aka—knowledge); it is also rule and authority (aka—kingdom). This same John also heard him say, "I am the Alpha and Omega, the beginning and the ending" (Rev 1:8). So, once again there you have it, "In the divine Logos or Word, God created the heavens and the earth."

The beloved apostle John continues to write, ". . .and the Word was with God, and the Word was God" (John 1:1). This is where some theologians with great effort attempt to make a distinction between God and the Word by emphasizing the word 'with' to prove the deity and person of Jesus Christ. Make no mistake, I agree to the deity and person of Christ, as the Word became flesh (word–made–man) and dwelt among us. However, some scholars make this separation at the expense of altering the meaning of this passage and missing altogether how God himself relates to the Logos. I had heard it said that the Logos or Word is "God reflecting upon himself." When I heard that, it was like finding the missing piece of a puzzle. Yet for the best of me, I could not initially validate the notion with scripture, until now after considerable contemplation by the blessed spirit of truth.

The text says the Word was *with* God. There are a few different ways in which "with" is used in the New Testament scriptures. One means together or to be in "sync" as a sense to be with one another as partners. Another is to be alongside as in a side–by–side relationship. However, John uses a different Greek word here which gives the meaning of "face–to–face." Now what we have is this Word or Logos, this divine logic and reasoning, this idea was face–to–face to God.

I would have you to understand that it was not something outside of himself but rather God reflecting upon himself. Just as we may reflect upon ourselves, God was reflecting and considering himself. I would dare to say that Spirit was reflecting upon his very own soul or expression. This was not two separate independent parts of God but rather two contained in the one. This was not something apart from God but rather within him. This was not a separate personal power in addition to God but rather very much God himself. The Word of God was the idea of God and vice–versa. The Word is a divine aspect of God, yet not something less than God. It is not a subset of God but rather his divine logic and percepts. Therefore, the phrase "the

Word was with God" is his own reflection upon himself, God face-to-face with himself.

This may lend a better understanding to John's next statement "the Word was God." Now a linking verb is used in the phrase "Word was God" and is therefore reversible. We can say the "Word was God" and "God was the Word." Just as your logic, thoughts and expression are you, this Word was and is very much God. We can say that God faced his own divine logic, it was his own contemplation of himself, his very own conscience. The Word was God's own understanding of himself. It is from within himself in which creation originated. This would make 'The Word' the original divine matrix of introspect and expression. It can be said that the "Word was with God" as well as the "Logos was face-to-face God." Likewise, it can be said the "Word was God" or the "divine idea of God." Said another way, the divine Logos is Christ the original matrix!

Consider, the very idea of creation in the mind of God! Should it surprise us that such a magnificent thing as the creation of the heavens and earth was first in the mind of God? In order that great cities are to be built, first the architect must have the blueprints or plans of the city in mind. Aircraft and ships have blueprints and computing systems have a detailed design before they are built. To simply start building without planning is disorderly and would lead to chaos. God is the divine architect of the universe, and Moses gives us a glimpse into how God created the universe, how he first planned. Such a fascinating idea to even consider, that God had this in his own mind followed by the act itself of creating it, and Moses gives us the story!

But before proceeding with the account in Genesis, there is more to consider about the Word of God. We read the Psalmist saying, "By the word of the LORD were the heavens made" (Ps 33:6). The heavens were made by the Logos, the divine logic, the very idea and reasoning of God. To assume that the Psalmist meant the spoken word is to assume poorly. Saint Augustine stated that it was by the sheer command of God that all of creation came into existence. He called it the divine imperative or fiat. Although it is true that much did come into existence by this mode, God did not create everything by this manner. Simply read the account of Genesis and you will discover that the greatest of God's creations were not by speaking them into existence but rather *made* by the work of God. Such include the heavens, the earth, the sun, the moon, the stars and even man himself.

The Word of God made all things and if anything was made, it was by the divine Logos. This is confirmed by John when he said, "All things were made by him; and without him was not anything made that was made" (John 1:3). Likewise, Paul tells us, "For by (in) him were all things created"

(Col 1:16), speaking of he who was the image of the invisible God and first-born of every creature. This indicates that both Paul and John recognized Christ as being that Word of God, the divine Logos from heaven. Indeed, he was the divine man or ideal man which took on the form of humanity and walked among us, the full revelation and expression of grace and truth.

We simply do not easily understand this Word of God as did early thinkers, however Paul understood it quite well. In fact, and most interestingly, seldom did Paul refer to Jesus as the man who walked the streets of Galilee. Yet this idea of the Logos or Word of God seem to have absorbed Paul's mind and dominated his thoughts. This man Jesus was now risen and exalted. He could not be separated from his divine origin, essence and being, and to Paul, this Christ was the divine Logos or Word of God.

Once again, theologian R.J. Campbell indicated that Paul knew he was living his life in vital relationship to the divine man of pre-Christian thought and experience. He said that this divine man was held to be that side or expression of the being of God from which the finite universe and all mankind have come forth. He goes on to point out that this thought is also found in that great apocalyptic book of Daniel which was written during the period of the Maccabee insurrection. It matters little how we regard the story, whether as history or as allegory, or partly one and partly the other, so long as we learn the lesson. We find in this book the figurative story of Shadrach, Meshach and Abednego and how they were cast into the fiery furnace for not worshipping the image set by King Nebuchadnezzar. This story, albeit parabolic, was told with intense dramatic influence upon the listener. Campbell continued to say that the story goes on to speak of four men loose in the fire and none having been hurt. It is said that the fourth is like a son of God and speaks directly to the concept of the divine man, the architect of humankind and the entire universe.[2]

I must insist, if we are willing to consider it, that this must have been one of Paul's greatest discoveries, as he was not ignorant of the Graeco-Jewish (union of Greek thought with Hebrew religion) models of the divine man. Consider it again, the side or expression of God in which is the source of all of humanity is the divine man; it is the ideal Logos; it is the Word. The Greek Logos doctrine of the being of God and his operation in the world was popular among Greek thinkers of this time: The idea of God expressing himself in the Logos by which creation and all that it contains had come into being.

As for Paul, this divine man in his full expression was Christ. For Paul, Jesus Christ was every bit the promised Messiah and equally every bit that

2. Campbell, *New Theology Sermons*, 6–7

divine man from heaven and side expressed as the Word. Jesus was all that was meant by the ideal manhood and much more. Just considering the fusion of the experience and presence of the spirit of Jesus with the idea of the Greek Logos must have been revolutionary to the apostle. Indeed, the Word made flesh!

Paul understood that man belonged to God because of this archetypical man, the divine Logos to whom all men belong and whose life is the light of man. Make no mistake, Paul was not indicating Jesus was merely the embodiment of heavenly manhood, but rather Jesus Christ was the divine man himself, the Word of God. As such, we find Paul relating so often to this risen and exalted Christ. This is perhaps why he could say, "henceforth we know no man after the flesh. Yea, though we have known Christ himself after the flesh, yet now henceforth we know him no more" (2 Cor 5:16).

4

The Word of God

THE APOSTLE OF LOVE, John the revelator makes this remarkable statement, "and his name is called The Word of God" (Rev 19:13).

I am sure most realize that this is not to be understood as his surname such as Mr. Word. Names are interesting in scripture. We know that a name can often imply a nature. As Christians, God has given us a new name and that is a spiritual name, not a new natural name. He has given us a new or renewed and reconstructed nature. In the Bible, we find that God had changed some names. For example, Abram was renamed Abraham and his wife Sarai to Sarah. Additionally, we find Jacob renamed to Israel, Simon to Peter and the sons of Zebedee to sons of thunder. We also find multiple names for some in scripture as it was customary for the Hebrews to use two or three names. Likewise, Saul (of Tarsus) is used nearly two dozen (less one) times and his name Paul is used well over a hundred times. There are many other examples in scripture. Suffice it to say, a name means something important and implies the nature of the person in many cases, oftentimes the natural circumstances and reasoning for the name (e.g., Sarah said God made her to laugh, thereby Abraham called his son Isaac).

I am reminded of the time when my two children were perhaps eleven and nine years old, and we were taking the automobile through a car wash. While in the wash, my daughter asked me, "Dad why did you and Mom name me Nicole?" I replied that we had a book with names for children and had begun looking through the book, starting with the letter "A." Eventually, we became tired by the time we got to the middle of the book. So, we stopped there and picked a name in the middle of the alphabet. Of course, we had already had a few names selected prior to flipping through the book and I was teasing her. Then my son asked the same question regarding his name. I replied, we did the same in choosing your name, that is, looking through the book starting with an "A" and growing weary. His name is Austin.

A new name? This should not be understood that we are simply to receive another name that is spelled and pronounced differently. I have met several that think such a foolish thought. I am reminded of the words of that great theologian, poet and writer of the nineteenth-century, George MacDonald, who was also considered by C.S. Lewis as his mentor. He said, "The true name is one that expresses the character, the nature, the being, the *meaning* of the person who bears it. It is the man's own symbol, his soul's picture, in a word, the sign which belongs to him and to no one else. Who can give a man this, his own name? God alone. For no one, but God sees what the man is, or even, seeing what he is, could express in a name-word the sum and harmony of what he sees. To whom is this name given? To him that overcometh. When is it given? When he has overcome," and "Such a name cannot be given until the man is the name."[1]

Regarding Jesus Christ, his name is called the Word of God. In other words, his nature was the divine Logos of God. Perhaps this is the reason he could say (paraphrase), "if you have seen me, you have seen the One that sent me." He was the perfect revelation of God himself for he was the Word in human form, the express image of his essence. The Christ himself was the very Word of God, the divine and ideal man from heaven! And yet, the irony is that he lowered himself from his former glory to take on humanity and experience becoming a man, taking on human nature.

The Puritans and Quakers disputed over the phrase "Word of God" hundreds of years ago. The former held the Word of God was the Bible while the latter held that this high and exalted title belongs to Christ and him alone. When I read, "For the Word of God is quick, and powerful, and sharper than any two-edged sword, piercing even to the dividing asunder of soul and spirit, and of the joints and marrow, and is a discerner of the thoughts and intents of the heart" (Heb 4:12), it becomes apparent that it can only be the Word of God that liveth and abideth forever, the divine Logos from eternity, the Christ whose name is called the Word of God. It is this Word that can truly divide between my soul and spirit and discern my

---

1. MacDonald, *Unspoken Sermons*, 41

heart. Paul did not intend for this verse to refer to the Bible, as mistakenly understood. To Paul, the divine Logos from eternity, the indwelling Christ was that discerner of soul and spirit.

The Word of God existed long before the scriptures. Indeed, the book called the Bible are sacred writings of God's people throughout history. It is where we can find how God in times past had revealed himself to his people and how they came to tell their story of his revelation in their lives. It is their witness of the true and living God within the time and culture in which they were written. It conveys inspired thoughts by various people in order that others may learn, come to understand, be corrected, be inspired themselves and establish teachings. Yet, the Bible is not the Christ, rather it is the story of Jesus Christ. It testifies of him who is the true abiding Word. It contains the sacred unfolding of God's ways and points to Christ. It is the greatest book known to man. In a particular manner, it certainly can be thought of as the written Word of God as people were inspired and told their stories, eventually to be scribed. In this sense, the Bible is not like any other book.

The Bible did not become flesh and dwell among us. The Bible will neither save me nor you, though the One in whom it speaks most certainly can—Jesus Christ the Word of God. I dare to say, even though we tend to think of such things as the spoken Word and the written Word, however there is only one Word, not two. There is not a greater and a lesser Word, namely non-written and written.

The American pastor/teacher/writer Brian Zahnd has said, "John the Baptist was sent by God, but John was not God. John bore witness to the Word, but John was not the Word. John was inspired by God, but John was not God incarnate. This is how we should understand the relationship between the Bible and the revelation of God in Christ . . . John the Baptist and the Bible play similar roles in relation to the eternal Logos who is Christ. We might say it this way: 'There was a book sent from God, whose name was the Bible. It came as a witness to the light, so that all might believe through it.' The Bible testifies through John the Baptist. Jesus is he of whom I said, 'He who comes after me ranks ahead of me because he was before me.' This is not a low view of Scripture but a high view of Christ."[2]

The twentieth century, once Catholic Priest turned Charismatic Protestant, Giuseppe Petrelli wrote, "Another necessary advice: namely of not falling into the error that every doctrine and development is to be found in the Bible. Let us explain. The Bible is the most precious book, the Book of books; but it only briefly alludes to themes, without unfolding them, for it is the Holy Spirit, and not the Book, Who must pilot the Church. The Holy

2. Zahnd, *Sinners in the Hands of a Loving God*, 29–30

Spirit uses the book as a witness. That it is so clearly inferred by what is written in Saint John 20:30–31, and 21:25. Very little is written, but enough has been recorded to enable man to begin. Moreover, no volume or library could ever contain all that Jesus did. We are in the Infinite. And the Holy Spirit brings us to the Infinite."[3]

Therefore, if we reduce the Word or divine Logos to a book, we run into all sorts of problems and entirely miss the point. The Bible is not "the Word of God" but it is "a word of God" and it informs us of the Word of God, the divine Logos, the Eternal Christ.

What we have in Genesis is that this Word, this beginning, this divine understanding of God, this original idea was something within himself. This divine matrix was the reflection of God whereby originated his creation. It is here that Moses shows us what God was reflecting upon, first the organized plan in his mind, the idea(s) of creation. Moses masterfully demonstrates that the divine Being is both Father and Creator of the universe, "In the beginning God created the heaven and the earth. And the earth was without form, and void; and darkness was upon the face of the deep. And the Spirit of God moved upon the face of the waters." God creates! This creation process was unfolding in the mind of God. But what does he create from? Theologians have long indicated God created "ex nihilo." This is a Latin phrase meaning "out of nothing." In other words, God created out of nothing. Unlike an artist that creates by using the various mediums of paint provided him, God had nothing outside of himself from which to draw upon to create, therefore, out of nothing external. Yet, he did have something, for He created out of himself, from his very own substance, not out of nothing. You see, you can only get nothing out of nothing for it is *no–thing*. So, God in his infinite wisdom produced something out of himself. This is not to be confused with Pantheism that everything is part of God, yet we find that God generated from within himself, and out of the "Word," he creates! Out of the Word, the original matrix, God expresses and unfolds his very idea of creation.

God conceived creation in his own mind. He prototypes or models the heavens (plural) and the earth. Then Moses describes the earth, not yet the heavens. He says the earth was without form and void. The world was void and vacant (Moffatt translation); the earth existed waste and void (Young's Literal); the earth became chaos and vacant (Concordant Literal). But what does it mean without form? I can't imagine or picture formlessness? Such an image would not have any shape for my mind to capture. It also carries the idea of desolation, of vanity and nothingness, as well as worthless and

3. Petrelli, *Heavenward*, 201–202

confusion. And what does it mean to be void? To be empty or emptiness, undistinguishable ruin, void. The early church father and great theologian Origen wrote, "And the earth was invisible, disordered and darkness was upon the abyss, and the Spirit of God moved over the waters."[4] First as an idea, an invisible earth before it comes into material existence; God determined to create the visible world, but first he modeled it as an idea, in the Logos, as he reflected upon himself.

And the earth was void, disordered with darkness upon it. Figuratively, misery, death, ignorance, sorrow, and obscurity was upon it, lacking understanding. This emptiness and darkness was upon the face of the deep or the abyss. Darkness was filling every empty space.

I often wonder how God may have brought forth creation. Some would suggest he created the earth perfect and it 'became' chaos over time. That is perhaps the case, but maybe it occurred differently. Is it possible that God, when projecting himself, he held something back, as if he withheld light, understanding or illumination? God's idea in modeling the earth was to first withhold something, to withhold himself, if you will, thereby we find darkness or absence of light, the privation of his presence and goodness, thereby darkness and evil, or "non–being." Yet, God is light and in him is no darkness at all. So, what does God then do? What would you expect a dark–less God to do? Not a demanding Zeus type god with his hurling lightning bolts, but a creative perfect God. He moves! He does not remain idle. The Spirit of God then hovers, flutters, or vibrates over the face of the deep.

Then, out of his precise orchestrated movement, he issues the divine imperative, God utters his command, "Let there be light: and there was light." Now, according to Moses, the creation of the natural sun was not until the fourth day. Here we find God announcing light, and it was so. God speaks light, understanding or illumination into creation. This is not the creation of light, it is "uncreated" light for God is light. It would not be possible to not have light at any time, or before. Therefore, this uncreated light is the light of God which has always been. Reading our text verse closely, He did not create light but rather spoke it into the void. Yet, this uncreated light would only be perceptible to the spirit as it filled the void to which it was spoken. Likewise, we now have the blueprint for the natural sun.

Next, we have that God saw that the light was good. It was the light, not the darkness that was good. We ought not make the mistake of thinking everything has some intrinsic goodness to it. We see here the beginning phases of how illumination would dispel ignorance. But God did not completely eradicate darkness, and for this reason God distinguishes the

---

4. Origen, *Homilies on Genesis and Exodus*, 47

darkness from light by dividing it, by separating it and putting a barrier or wall, by placing boundaries between the two—light and darkness. What are these boundaries? He called the light Day, and darkness he called Night. Here, he places an order to it, "And the evening and the morning were the first day," more accurately, they were one day. Should it surprise us that he divided or that he would separate? He prevents a clashing by dividing it. He keeps them from constant contact by placing an order. However, when light comes, darkness retreats and yields to it.

Paul saw that there was an allegorical aspect to this account in Genesis that parallels the experience of the spiritual birth of the believer. He stated that "God, who commanded the light to shine out of darkness, hath shined in our hearts . . ." (2 Cor 4:6). Just as God commanded light to shine out of darkness, God has shined in our hearts. He spoke into our ignorance and lack of understanding, our alienation and darkness, and he gives light, understanding and illumination. He gives the "light of the knowledge of the glory of God in the face of Jesus Christ." Out of the invisible, the unreachable, the unsearchable, the very God of creation that is concealed reveals himself and speaks the uncreated light into our darkened soul. This spark illuminates and penetrates our minds, the uncreated light of knowledge shining forth to help us understand our identity in relation to the divine Logos and our true destiny, which is the image and likeness of God.

5

In His Image

"AND GOD SAID, LET us make man in our image, after our likeness: and let them have dominion over the fish of the sea, and over the fowl of the air, and over the cattle, and over all the earth, and over every creeping thing that creepeth upon the earth. So God created man in his image, in the image of God created he him: male and female created he them" (Gen 1:26–27).

Moses informs us that God announced what he was about to do—make man in our image, "after our likeness." The word "image" means a reflection, a visual impression of something as in a mirror, a copy, a mental picture or idea, a representation of a person or thing. Strong's concordance of the original Hebrew provides the meaning of resemblance, representative figure, form or phantom. So, man was created in the image or resemblance of his creator!

God is Spirit, is he not? So, God creates a man in his image, first and foremost a spiritual man! Have you ever noticed in verse twenty–seven that it did not continue to say that man was created after God's likeness? I dare say, I think it was not by accident that it was omitted, but rather intentional. Now understand that this perfect image must take form or expression, whereby man is then made in the "likeness" of God. The original word for "likeness" means fashion, after the manner or similitude, model or shape.

Therefore, our text verse could easily read, "Let us make man in our resemblance and after our similitude."

So, man was created in the image of God, from the same essence or substance of his heavenly Father. Out of and through the very divine of God himself, the eternal Logos or that aspect from which humanity originates, man is created. Using idioms, he was a chip off the old block, a dead ringer, or the spitting image of his Father.

That wonderful early church father Gregory of Nyssa (AD 335—394) said, "In what then does the greatness of man consist, according to the doctrine of the Church? Not in his likeness to the created world, but in his being in the image of the nature of the Creator."[1]

Listen again to the words of Moses, "And the Lord God formed man of the dust of the ground and breathed into his nostrils the breath of life; and man became a living soul" (Gen 2:7). God breathed into man "the breath of" life. This was not merely giving man the ability to breath oxygen, thereby simply possessing animal or biological life.

First, we find in scripture that "the spirit of" man is the candle of the Lord (Prov 20:27). Likewise, "but there is a spirit in man: and 'the inspiration' of the Almighty giveth them understanding" (Job 32:8). These phrases "the breath of," "the spirit of," and "the inspiration" come from the same Hebrew word. It could easily read in Genesis 2:7 that God breathed into man's nostrils inspired life or spirit life. In other words, that which was deposited into man was spirit and it was divine inspiration. It was man's illumination, a candle that shines and brightens, providing light. It should be easy to understand that the divine inspiration (the spirit) of man is the illumination (candle) of the Lord. To suggest otherwise is to reject the witness of the spirit and the testimony of scripture.

Second, this single word for "life" in this verse means to be alive or have existence. Any attempt to make a distinction of the type of life from this single word without its use of supporting adjectives or surrounding context would be an exercise of futility. For example, it would be fool hearted to suggest that this merely means man's biological life and not inspiration from God. We can agree with the observation that creatures were alive and had existence. However, we must not overlook the fact that this same word "life" is found numerous times as God "liveth." Clearly one would be hard pressed to conclude that "liveth" refers to the biological life of God. Furthermore, we read of the tree of "life" in the midst of the garden. Again, the same can be supposed that this is a physical biological literal tree of "life" while holding to childhood fables of an apple, a physical talking snake and hanging fruit

1. Gregory of Nyssa, *On The Making of Man*, 404

called good and evil. Suffice it to say, the existence of man far exceeded biological life, it was the inspired life of God.

This is where we find God placing his very own substance and being into man. This is where we discover God creating out of that aspect of himself, the divine Logos, to image himself into his greatest creation. This is where we find that man is created in the image of God!

Hear the words of that prolific writer—J. Preston Eby, with whom I had the privilege and honor to spend some time. "What God actually did was that he imaged himself in man. God imaged himself in man by forming himself in a man of earth. Thus man was created as a visible expression of the invisible God," and ". . .the very being of man has a God–ward or divine side, being related constitutionally to Him," and again, "The word 'spirit' means literally, breath, and denotes a quality of life because, in the case of the spirit of man, God is able to breath himself into it and through it. The word 'inspiration' as used here, denotes the act of inbreathing. Anyone who is inspired is 'breathed into', visited internally by the power of life, and so quickened in mind, raised in intelligence, ennobled in nature, and empowered in ability."[2]

We can finally connect the dots. This explains precisely when and where God created man in his image. The divine essence of life was placed inside man, it was part of his make–up or configuration and man became a living soul. Not just a creature that had breath, not as the beasts of the field, but he was inspired from within via the image, and he therefore lived and moved and had his being in God. He was in the image of God as he originated from his creator, as something would proceed out of a matrix, yet far more dynamic and personal. Given that man was of the same essence and substance, of the same stuff, it should not be difficult to understand that God did something quite unique within man, unlike the other creatures. He created man out of the divine Logos and imaged himself into man.

Gregory of Nyssa makes the distinction between the created nature of man and the uncreated nature of God in his magnificent writing, "*On The Making of Man.*" Now, I take an unorthodox position on this matter and I believe it is an extremely important point that ought not be missed. The common view is that Christ is eternal and uncreated while humanity is neither. If there is a vast distinction between Christ and us, it begs the question of how we are truly following the pattern. The point is exactly this, we share something in common, and it is the "uncreated Logos," the out–breathing of God, the very being of God imaged as the spirit of man, placed inside the created man. This is perhaps the greatest revelation that Jesus brought to humanity, to become what we are!

2. Eby, *The Seed in Every Man*, 2–3

We are in a sense a portion of the eternal divine substance, or as Paul said, "as certain also of your own poets have said, for we are also his off-spring" (Acts 17:28). This is where we can better understand that humanity has its noble origin from God himself, traced back to Adam and called a son of God. This is where we can better understand that God imaged himself in man, the divine Logos, the eternal Christ in man.

God placed his very own image, a part or portion of himself into man, albeit this is not to fragment or divide God as we struggle to find the correct words to explain the placing of his resemblance into man. Therefore, in the totality of man's framework, he consists of his *body* wherein he comes into contact with his external surroundings, where he finds expression on this physical plane, where man would be world–conscious; of his *soul* comprised of his will, intellect, emotions from senses, personality and expression, whereby he could be self–conscious; and his *spirit*, the uncreated image breathed into him wherein he could desire, reason, reflect upon and commune with his creator and father out of his very own being, thereby being God–conscious.

It is man as a whole person that is in union with his creator, not his individual parts. I believe it quite important to understand that man was created both with a human–element (body and soul) and god–like–element (divine image). Man called to express his heavenly father, to be an image-bearer of life from the divine source of his very innermost being.

I once read an article in the National Geographic magazine about the Antarctic Ocean. I recall it saying that if you were to look across this Ocean, as far as the eye can see, you would see nothing but a vast whiteness. Everything would appear to be dormant, no activity, no life. But the writer of the article went on to say, when you look underneath that ice, whether it is twelve inches, twenty–four inches, thirty–six inches or more, there is such vitality, and a proliferation of life taking place underneath that large sheet of ice. The article went on to suggest there is more activity in that Ocean than all the other Oceans put together (the Pacific, the Atlantic, the Indian and so forth). Now, I must admit, when I read this article, I was fascinated with the information that I had otherwise known nothing about. At that moment it dawned upon me that this is the way it is in the Spirit, the inner man that is renewed day by day. We may not always observe it with our senses (sight, hear, smell, taste or touch), but nevertheless, it is true. Oftentimes, we think that all is dormant, having little to no activity, yet rest assured, we have this inner man, the Christ in the very depths of our being mightily at work, an inner life that lives inside of us.

Just as much as it is true that your physical tabernacle (tent) or body is perishing day by day, likewise the soul that desires the external world or outward man continues to perish, yet the inner man is renewed day by day. Paul said, "and though our outward man perish, yet the inward man is renewed day by day" (2 Cor 4:16).

First and foremost, he was spiritual, a man made in the image of God. The apostle Paul stated that man "is the image and glory of God" (1 Cor 11:7). Have you ever considered that *man is the image and glory* of God? God created Adam in his own image, he was a son of God and he communed with God in the spirit (cool) of the day. Yet, Adam had lost that image with the fall, that reflection and representation of his creator and father.

Listen to the parable of the woman and the lost coin. I shall paraphrase the story and use it as an application to illustrate our text verse. It is a story of a woman and the image of a coin. The coin is lost inside her own house. Therefore, she lights a candle, sweeps the house, and seeks diligently till she finds the coin and rejoices with her friends that the coin had been found. When describing the soul through scripture, it is often referred to in the feminine gender. So, can you not see how our soul is likened unto the woman in this story and has lost something as well? The woman lost a coin which would have an imprinted image on it. Likewise, our soul has lost the image in which it was originally created in God. So, the woman lights a candle before beginning her search. Likewise, the spirit of man is the candle of the Lord and requires illumination to begin its own discovery. Now, we find that the woman does not look outside of her house but rather inside, *within* her house. Again, we seek diligently for that missing coin or valuable image that has been lost to us. Where are we to find that missing image? Outside of ourselves, spatially? No, but rather deep down *within* our soul, where the image of the divine can be found. Therein lies the mystery and revelation, the divine Logos–man, made in the very image of God.

It is certainly true of our own experience as Paul stated, "As we have borne the image of the earthy, we shall also bear the image of the heavenly" (1 Cor 15:49). Indeed, our soul has borne the image of the carnality and outward man, always seeking the exterior or outward for her satisfaction. Yet we are to bear the image of the heavenly. Our soul is to be spiritual, bearing the image of the inner man that is renewed day–by–day, and when we do experience those moments of refreshing, finding that lost coin, taking on the image and glory of God, we rejoice with our friends.

Perhaps the greatest scholar that the Catholic church has ever had, Hans Urs von Balthasar, wrote the following, ". . .the image that, according to the theologians, man finds inscribed in his being and that he is supposed to develop through gradual ascent into a likeness with God is a clear borrowing from the Greek idea of *homoiosis* (assimilation). Paul's citation from Aratus in his discourse at the Areopagus (Acts 17:28) is yet another piece of evidence pointing to the same conclusion. Biblically speaking, the idea that man is God's image remains insignificant until Christ appears in our midst as the archetype who re-creates our former man (Rom 8:29) and renewed in the knowledge after the image of his creator (Col 3:10)."[3]

We are discovering that we have been made in the image of God, and it is changing our thoughts, both the perception of ourselves as well as others. Certainly, this has been hidden from us. It has been covered by so much that shapes our experience (sorrow, pain, hurt, shame, sin, etc.), yet this inner reality is there. We do not deny that such things obstruct, but none of them constitute our higher self. They only obscure it. Beloved Theophilus, we are to know that God imaged himself into our very make-up, and though we have been unconscious and detached from the very source of life, our soul is awakening to its divine origin and place in God.

3. Balthasar, *Man is Created*, 18–19

6

After His Likeness

GOD CREATED MAN IN his own image and then began to form or shape man after his likeness, experience by experience, all within each day. Man would be molded and shaped through the crucible of the day, both evening and morning, of the interplay of night (darkness) and day (light) happenings.

So, God created a spiritual man in his image and then formed, fashioned or made him in his likeness. But when did God do this? It says, "In the day that God created man, in the likeness of God made he him" (Gen 5:1). At first glance, one may think that man was both created and made in his likeness at the same precise moment. In fact, it says they both occurred *in the day.* God said to man "in the day that thou eatest thereof, thou shalt surely die" (Gen 2:17), or as the Concordant Literal translation states "dying, you shall die." However, Adam lived for 930 years, as a day is a thousand years with the Lord, and a thousand years a day. Therefore, it was within this same timeframe of *a day,* (during man's lifespan, 930 years in Adam's case), that God molded, formed, fashioned, made in his likeness or similitude— his created man.

God made man in his likeness, but what is man? I suppose it could be difficult to answer the question without first having an idea of what, or more appropriately, who is God? What I mean by this is that one's concept and notion of God will certainly influence his view of man, both of himself and humanity. If one's view of God is noble, then such will find nobility in mankind. If kindness or forgiveness, then such shall be found in others as well. If judgmental and condemning, again the same disposition shall eventually be dealt to others.

The Psalmist asked, "When I consider thy heavens, the work of thy fingers, the moon and the stars, which thou hast ordained; What is man, that thou art mindful of him? And the son of man, that thou visitest him? For thou hast made him a little lower than the angels, and hast crowned him with glory and honour. Thou madest him to have dominion over the works of thy hands; thou hast put all things under his feet" (Ps 8:3–6). Isn't it amazing that God would create such a creature and be mindful of or thinking upon him, always remembering him? In the original, it says He made him a little lower than the ELOHIM, while the Moffatt translation states a little less than divine (meaning the divine God). Indeed, man is the greatest creation of God, exceeding the earth, the sun, the moon, the stars and the heavens, as well as above that which was spoken into existence.

It has been said that man is a universe within a universe. Many have tried to figure out the outer universe, which in honest pursuit can only lead back to discovering more of its creator—God. The universe is God's own thought of himself expressed, which is unending, eternal, and infinite. But what of the inner universe, namely man? If only we could see man as God sees him! If we could understand the story of man as God has written it, we would understand more of God. To understand his created humanity, we then may begin to understand its creator.

Man, not merely as he thinks of himself, but man as God thinks of him, is all that really matters. In spite of all man's wrongdoing, the terrible wickedness and sin, the imperfections and woes, dare we even suggest that we are to look for something greater, more noble, more loving, more divine? To which with the utmost confidence, I say a thousand times over "Amen."

We are being molded and shaped after the manner or similitude of Christ himself, made after his likeness. When we do this, we align to the thoughts of Paul when he said, "And have put on the new man, which is renewed in knowledge after the image of him that created him: Where there is neither Greek nor Jew, circumcision nor uncircumcision, Barbarian, Scythian, bond nor free: but Christ is all, and in all. Put on therefore, as the elect of God, holy and beloved, bowels of mercies, kindness, humbleness of mind, meekness, longsuffering; Forbearing one another, and forgiving one another, if any man have a quarrel against any: even as Christ forgave you, so also do ye. And above all these things put on charity, which is the bond of perfectness. And let the peace of God rule in your hearts . . ." (Col 3:10–15).

When we do this, our perspective is rightly aligned, "For as he thinketh in his soul, so is he" (Pro 23:7).

This image can be none other than the divine Logos, the expression and being of God from which humanity came forth. We learned earlier that Christ is the very Word of God, and it is this very image that is being formed in us, imprinted into our very soul, to be found after his likeness, capturing every thought and making what was once wrong, now right. Or as the apostle Peter reminds us, that we are "called to glory and virtue . . . that . . . ye might be partakers of the divine nature" (1 Pet 1:4).

Prior to receiving the law from Moses, the children of Israel were without any Word, yet Moses bore that image and delivered it to them. We find John the Baptist saying of the Word made flesh, "He that cometh after me is preferred before me: for he was before me." With that in mind, he continues to say; "Because out of the fulness of him we all received, and favor upon favor. For the law was given through Moses, but grace and truth came through Jesus Christ" (John 1:15–17).

Here we find John the Baptist saying that the Word existed long before himself, and then he states of his fullness we (that is—our own people) have received, favor and truth as it was given through (not "by") Moses, to give us the law. John the Baptist understood that Moses administered the law through that divine Logos which he possessed. Certainly, Moses was not without fault, but that is not our emphasis at this moment. Rather this Moses did God send to be a ruler and a deliverer (ransom) for Israel. His ransom was not to Egypt; he paid them nothing. It was his own life which he poured out for Israel, freely giving of his life for them. Indeed, Moses face-to-face with God (Exod 33:11). Peter affirms this regarding the prophets when he said, "the Spirit of Christ which was *in them* did signify . . ." (1 Pet 1:9). Note: emphasis mine.

Even Christian orthodoxy affirms that since Christ has identified himself wholly with every man, in every one of his sad and most sorrowful states, the person who "does it to the least of his brethren" does it to Christ himself, not "as if" to Christ, but to Christ in reality, for Christ is most truly within every man, and every man is the bearer of Christ, the image of the invisible God.

Further considering the image, it reminds me of the making of the statue of David by one of the greatest artists in the history of the world, Michelangelo of Florence, Italy. The marble statue represents the biblical David. Unveiled in the Fall of 1504, it is said that the 26-year old Michelangelo worked on the already badly blocked and incomplete David (neglected for many years), started the challenging task in the Fall of 1501. Imagine the block of marble concealed from the public, as the gifted sculptor erected his shack and covering it, began with his hammer and chisel, morning and evening, laboring to bring forth that beautiful image that had captured his mind. As I considered this illustration, it dawned upon me that the image that the sculptor labored towards was already there embedded in the stone waiting to be revealed. His chisel was to carve out, scrape away and remove everything except the actual image. Such an image could not be formed, shaped, molded or made in the likeness—as if it were clay. He was removing the unnecessary outward stone that concealed and entombed the inward image of David.

Paul understood this concept of unveiling when he said, "But when it pleased God, who separated me from my mother's womb, and called me by his grace, to reveal (unveil) his Son in me, that I might preach him among the heathen . . ." (Gal 1:15). Notice that he didn't say, when it pleased God to put his Son into my heart, but rather to unveil, uncover, *apokalupto* his Son in me. This was the mystery hidden from ages and generations, and Paul testified, " . . . but now is made manifest to the saints: To whom God would make known what is the riches of the glory of this mystery among the Gentiles; which is Christ in you, the hope of glory" (Col 1:26–27). This is the eternal Christ, the divine Logos, the image of God.

Furthermore, Paul informs us "But, we all, with open face beholding as in a glass the glory of the Lord, are changed into the same image from glory to glory, as by the Spirit of the Lord" (2 Cor 3:18). Certainly, by revelation it is the Lord himself that transforms us by bringing us into that image. But what does Paul mean when saying "beholding as in a glass" or we are "changed into the same image?" The "image" bears the idea of a statue, profile or as a coin having this image and superscription. Likewise, "changed" means to undergo a transformation—*metamorphose*. The Phillips translation reads, "We are transformed in ever–increasing splendor into his own image." But what would "as in a glass" mean or as other translations have stated, "reflect like mirrors?"

George MacDonald captured this wonderfully when he wrote: "Paul never thought of the mirror as reflecting, as throwing back the rays of light from its surface; he thought of it as receiving, taking into itself, the things presented to it—here, as filling its bosom with the glory it looks upon. When I see the face of my friend in a mirror, the mirror seems to hold it in itself, to surround the visage with its liquid embrace. The countenance is there, down there in the depth of the mirror. True, it shines radiant out of it, but it is not the shining out of it that Paul has in his thought; it is the fact—the visual fact, which . . . the poet always seizes, of the mirror holding in it the face." He goes on to say "Our mirroring of Christ, then, is one with the presence of his spirit in us. The idea, you see, is not the reflection, the radiating of the light of Christ on others, though that were a figure lawful enough; but the taking into, and having in us, him working to the changing of us."[1]

Similarly speaking, as the mirror has within itself that image, we have taken (albeit buried) that image of God into the depths of our soul. But it is not the taking of something from outside of ourselves, location–wise or spatially. Rather it is the taking into our very person that distant, lost and forgotten image that is already placed within us. Paul makes the beautiful connection to the ideal man, the divine Logos from heaven in its fullest revelation as Christ. Furthermore, he says, "until Christ be formed in you" (Gal. 4:19), or in other words, until the divine image be fully formed, shaped, fashioned, or imprinted into your soul–life, into the person of whom you were destined to be—made in his likeness!

Ignatius had the following to say, ". . . that two different characters are found among men—the one true coin, the other spurious. The truly devout man is the right kind of coin, stamped by God Himself. The ungodly man, again, is the false coin, unlawful, spurious, counterfeit, wrought not by God, but by the devil. I do not mean to say that there are two different human natures, but that there is one humanity, sometimes belonging to God, and sometimes to the devil. If anyone is truly religious, he is a man of God; but if he is irreligious, he is a man of the devil, made such, not by nature, but by his own choice. The unbelieving bear the image of the prince of wickedness. The believing possess the image of their Prince, God the Father, and Jesus Christ . . ."[2]

And what of our destiny? Paul said, "For whom he did foreknow, he also did predestinate to be conformed to the image of his Son, that he might be the firstborn among many brethren." (Rom 8:29) What a placing, what a calling, what a purpose, having been appointed and determined before the ages, unto glory, all which Paul indicates in his writings (e.g., Eph 1:5, Rom 8:30, Eph 1:11, 1 Cor 2:7). The doctrine of a pre–determined destiny or predestination was taught by Paul as well as his close companion Luke (see Acts 4:28). Unfortunately, this teaching has been often misunderstood through church history. Our destiny is not a place, nor for that matter are the subjects of heaven and hell even mentioned in any of the predestination verses. To the contrary, these statements have everything to do with our being destined to the conformity of the image of his Son, of Christ, of the divine Logos, that perfect ideal of man from heaven. In the eternal Christ we find our worth and identity.

1. MacDonald, *Unspoken Sermons*, 222–224
2. Ignatius, *Epistle of Ignatius to the Magnesians*, 61

I had the privilege of having met the gifted teacher, Ray Prinzing. On this topic of religion having two opposite or contrasting realms, he wrote, "'The heaven for height, and the earth for depth' (Prov 25:3). Interesting enough, it does not give tradition's contrast of heaven and hell, but rather, heaven and earth. Jesus Christ did not come to lead us from hell to heaven, He came to lead us from this earthly, carnal realm, to the Father. 'I am the way, the truth, and the life; no man cometh unto the Father, but by me' (John 14:6). Rather than being geographic locations, we can readily say that concerning both heaven and hell, they are 'a state or condition of being.' One songwriter beautifully stated it, 'Where Jesus is, tis heaven here,' for he was thinking of that harmony of fellowship and love. However, the Psalmist declared, 'If I make my bed in hell, behold, Thou art there' (Ps 139.8), for God's presence fills the universe. But to be aware of the presence of God, and yet to be out of fellowship and harmony with him, is indeed a hellish state. And this very earthly sojourn can become very much, a 'hell', if we are in rebellion to the will of God."[3] And may I add, perfect love casts out all fear.

Something can be said of the man that discovers, by the quickening of the Spirit of God, that he is made in the image of God. I found of interest what was said by the early church father Origen, "All men are born men, but we are not all men–men."[4] That expression *men–men* can be found in the original Hebrew, both by Moses and Ezekiel. For the inquiring mind, Ezekiel 14:4 says in the original, "Lord Adonai 'man–man' from the house of Israel," while Moses said, "Man–man of the house of Israel" (Lev 17:8). But is this just a play on words? Absolutely not. It speaks of the type of person we ought to be. Whether male or female, we are to be men–men, spiritually speaking. Not all are a *man–man*. Some are more bestial in their nature or beast–men (Ps 49:12), while some serpent–men (called vipers in scripture), so forth and so on.

So, what is the state or condition of our soul? Does it honor and reflect the image of the Word (divine Logos) or does it reflect another? Has it repented, changed direction, done a reversal, changed its trajectory, been arrest and turned about, changed mind or thought differently? Dare we ask ourselves, what type of men are we? I will tell you what we ought to be. We are to see in a mirror with our soul and have that inner man reflected, in all his splendor and glory. We are to show forth his attributes such as nobility, dignity, goodness, kindness, forgiveness, gentleness, compassion, love, mercy, and so on. We are to have a two–fold man displaying forth, both inner and outer.

3. Prinzing, *Redemption. . . All In All*, 41–42

4. Origen, *Homilies on Ezekiel*, 61–62

Paul did not think of Christ as one person and himself as completely another outside of him. His person embraced and was united with Christ as he said, "I am crucified with Christ: nevertheless I live; yet not I, but Christ liveth in me: and the life which I now live in the flesh I live by the faith of the Son of God, who loved me, and gave himself for me" (Gal 2:20). He understood salvation is secured by the union of his soul with the eternal Christ, the divine Logos, the divine man. As with Paul, there comes a time when God separates us from our mother's womb (spiritual Jerusalem), by his grace, to reveal his Son in us, in order to send us forth in the daily grind of life to set a groaning creation free, because our mother, which is above, is free, that heavenly Jerusalem, the womb of us all.

There comes a time where we are to possess our soul. Jesus said, "For what shall a man give in exchange for his soul" (Matt 8:37)? What a remarkable statement. Upon reviewing eighteen different translations, along with Strong's concordance, one might say verse 37 reads: What are we to give, bring forth, yield, offer . . . in exchange, an equivalent ransom . . . for our soul, our life? What is the price that we are to pay, in order to possess our soul?

That may be a new concept to the reader, that they are to pay something for their souls and that they have not always possessed their souls. Wait—I've been told my whole life Jesus paid the price, and I only need to accept it, mumble a few words, and like the thief on the cross, it's all mine for the getting, I am safe, covered, in! I thought it was as simple as name it and claim it, blab it and grab it, write a check, what the heck. Rub the genie bottle, wiggle my nose and poof.

What shall a man give in exchange for his soul? Here is what it is, I shall tell you. A two-souled man is unstable in all his ways. There aren't two distinct souls in a person but rather a lower-based soul and a higher spiritual soul (made in his likeness), yet one soul. The text says we are to give something that is equivalent, an exchange is to be made. I would suggest, it is soul for soul, the lower for the higher. I am to surrender and forfeit the desires of the lower-based soul, all its selfish tendencies in exchange for my redeemed soul, the higher soul life made in the likeness of Christ. This life is to be won, gained, sought after with all our seeking.

The greatest thing we can do for ourselves (and for others around us), is to *possess* our true souls. Most have never possessed their soul. In fact, many know not that it ought to be so! It will cost us everything, but the return on investment is well worth the price. May we find Christ possessing our soul-life!

7

The Humanity of the Divine

THE WRITER OF HEBREWS stated, "Who being the brightness of his glory, and the express image of his person . . ." (Heb 1:3). Jesus Christ was the divine Logos, the brightness of God's glory and the express image of his person. He was the exact copy or representation, having the engraved image imprinted or stamped upon himself, his resemblance and character. He was everything that the image of God was to be in a man. He was the long–awaited Messiah, and he was the ideal heavenly man from heaven.

He was the "image of the invisible God, the firstborn of every creature" (Col 1:15). He had been glorified with the Father's very own self, or as from his own lips, "And now, O Father, glorify thou me with thine own self with the glory which I had with thee before the world was" (John 17:5). Christ did not lay aside his divine nature, for that would have been an impossibility to separate himself from his identity and oneness with the very life of his existence. But he did "empty himself" and took upon himself the form of humanity.

We can never insist too much on the deity of Christ nor can we ever suggest too much on the humanity of Christ. The two natures combined perfectly together in union to be man in the person of Jesus Christ. Yet, there was not to be two consciousnesses in Christ, a divine and a human, but rather a divine–human consciousness, one and the same in perfect harmony. He is not either this or that, as turning one nature off momentarily, so order to function out of the other.

Frankly, many speak of humanity and divinity as though they are two different things, hoping one day that the twain shall meet, whenever and wherever that should be. But they are not two different things at all. They are one, non-separable, and undivided. In Jesus Christ these were not two natures cohabitating and in agreement with one another, but rather one perfect nature. His humanity was his divinity and his divinity his humanity. To think otherwise is to divide Christ. Dare we dissect and divide Christ into only human or solely divine, depending on how he conducted himself? To this, I would say, he is not to be separated.

Both the deity and humanity of Jesus Christ are fundamental principles to the Christian faith. In the fourth century, sometime before 318 AD, Arius of Alexandria had taught that Jesus Christ was not the pre–existent, eternally existing, uncreated person but rather a created being by God the Father. For Arius, God the Father created the divine Logos or Word as the first of his creation. This suggested that his view of a created–being–Word did not exactly have the same uncreated divine nature as God himself.

History tells us that this led to the largest gathering of church bishops (318 AD according to tradition) and the first ecumenical council in 325 AD in Nicea to settle the controversy, as ordered by Constantine. What exactly was decided at this gathering? In addition to the number of regulations or canons, these leaders of the church also decreed that the Logos–Word, the Son of God is uncreated, ever–existent and fully divine. They said he was generated, begotten or born from God the Father and not made or created by him. They additionally stated he was of one essence with the Father. We are also told the position of the Nicene council was not universally accepted for nearly five hundred years.

Another heresy arose in the fourth century disputing how Christ can be both divine and human at the same time. As such, a person named Apollinaris concluded that Jesus was not fully human. However, Gregory the Theologian objected, stating whatever belongs to human nature in which Jesus did not partake, then that facet of human nature could not have been saved!

Continuing with the history of the church as it relates to the nature of Christ, we find the second church council in the fourth century (381 AD) in Constantinople. Here they condemned the teachings of Arius and Apollinaris, along with some others, and reaffirmed the divinity of Christ. Forward winding to the fifth century, we find the third council of the church (431 AD) in Ephesus, again addressing many issues of contention, albeit not all issues were resolved—namely insisting on the term of "one nature" of the

Word of God incarnate or two natures. If it were insisted on one nature, the concern was Christ would not be seen fully human. And if two natures, the concern was not to over–emphasize his humanity, to the degree of it having its own independent existence which could lead to the false conclusion of two persons.

To no surprise, history bears out that further disputes continued this subject, which lead to the fourth great council in the fifth century (451 AD) in the city of Chalcedon, with over 630 bishops in attendance. The council upheld the divine and human natures of the former council's position of *hypostatic union*—which means the union of divinity and humanity in Christ. Certainly not our everyday word!

Among many things, this council defended Christ as the Logos incarnate, begotten of the Father before the ages, took to himself the whole of humanity and became a man in every way, yet never to sin. So, they concluded that Jesus Christ was fully divine and fully human. He was one person (hypostasis) in two natures, yet these were united without division, separation, changing or confusion. However, afterward, disputes continued over the terminology of "one nature" verse "two natures," as well as, the meaning of "union" or "unity."

Therefore, and for other schisms as well, in the sixth century we find the fifth church council (553 AD) in Constantinople. Here they declared that Christ was one and the same divine person who was united within himself, the two natures of humanity and divinity. They also indicated this was without fusing them together, meanwhile without allowing their separation in any way, shape, or form.

Therefore, the history of the church recognized the *hypostatic union* of the individual existence of Christ and the union of his humanity and divinity. The Athanasian Creed states, "Although he is God and human, yet Christ is not two, but one. He is one, however, not by his divinity being turned into flesh, but by God's taking humanity to himself. He is one, certainly not by blending of his essence, but by the unity of his person . . ." By some, this union is also referred as a *mystical union* and to its precise nature of the joining, it is beyond human comprehension.

Indeed, Jesus Christ, the God–Man, of one essence with all of humanity and of one essence with God the Father. The divine Logos, the Word made flesh, in perfect harmony within himself, is never simply a human, never only divine. Though it is understood and discussed in its formulas as two natures, I think it is far more appropriate to consider it as one nature in its incarnate state because of the unity of the natures, or as "two shall become one." This humanity of the divine was not the reproduction of change, as if the two came together to create a third nature. No, rather it is the completeness of the human and divine cooperating and functioning in its *togetherness*, a term that Karl Barth often used.

How does this come about in us? I think it most certainly must first come by revelation, an uncovering or discovery of truth. Furthermore, it is a realization of how we belong to God and what we mean to him, what we have always meant to him. Certainly, it is coming to know our Father, the God of the universe and source of all life. We gaze at the majestic wonder of the stars in the heavens, yet we know him to the degree of what we take into us in that moment. I see no more and no less, unless of course if he who is concealed decides to reveal himself more to me. So, we come hoping; we come expecting. Likewise, we come to that great divine matrix of humanity and . . . we find him there too! We find him in the beautiful baby, in the laughter of children, in the maturing of young adults, in the graceful aging and wisdom of the elderly and yes, even in the laughter of our fumbling through our spiritual journey.

I think of Jesus as a young boy, and his visit to the temple at the age of twelve, the consciousness of a child, yet so inclined to the business of his heavenly Father. His parents had trained him all his years, as was the custom of Jewish children, now sitting with the learned of the law, amazing them with his wisdom at such a young age; while he was still learning and growing as well. "Wist ye not that I must be about My Father's business" (Luke 2:49). Jesus, increasing in wisdom and stature, and in favor with God and man. We may find ourselves saying, "Oh that was Jesus, he was something far more special and different than the rest of humanity." Certainly, he had a super spiritual consciousness, whereas I could barely muster up such a thought when a child. But here is my point, God is the very same God, as he was to Jesus at age twelve. I would dare to say, you had the same consciousness of God, to a certain degree, as did Jesus when a boy. We simply did not increase in that wisdom as he.

I often wonder, certainly it is a wonderful thing when we know of our obedience and faithfulness in following his voice in the cool (spirit) of the day. In those moments of refreshing, I am sure we desire to hear those words, "Well done, thou good and faithful servant, enter into the joy of thy Lord." Certainly, that sounds like it ought to be enough, right? However, there is a spirit within my soul that desires to hear those words, "This is my beloved son, in whom I am well pleased."

What manner of man was this Jesus? He was always showing us the better way, the higher and more perfect way. I think of the beginning of his miracles. Such things as miracles strike men with astonishment, hoping to bring them to repentance. Miracles are signs of divine presence and activity; there are several cited in scripture, including those by Jesus himself. So, his beginning of miracles was at the marriage in Cana (John 2:1–11). We know the story quite well, as he turned the water into wine. But what of it? They had heard of miracles before and had believed the stories, yet no apparent change. Is there more to this story than simply another miracle for the Jewish people?

Giuseppe Petrelli wrote, "Every man is concerned in making a good impression at the beginning, not caring what happens in the end; but here the best was kept for the last, revealing a proceeding not common to men but to One alone. . . The new man keeps the best for the end." And again, "Every man, save the man, places the best first before presenting not only what is inferior but even the worst. Men wait until others have first lost their sense of proportion and even decency before offering the worst. The book of Revelation speaks of the dragon drawing a third part of the stars of heaven to earth with his tail. . . whose power to destroy is in the tails (Rev 9:10, 19; 12:4). The word *tail* is used to describe its effects. . . The lesson is clear. Every man, by identity of soul, gives the best that he has, knows, and is capable of first; he wants to appear generous and kind, and when he cannot, he does his best to save the appearance. This is the way every man acts. Only one man acted and acts differently."[1]

Is this not true of our own experience? Are we far too often at the end of a matter, found in our lower–base self, our carnal reasoning and digression from dignity and worth, running back to the swine for a season? We are lost once again, forgetting our true place in humanity, and finding the sting of death in the end, as the soul spirals downward. Still, God continues to call my higher self. He bids my soul to find its mystical union with Christ. Amen, to Jesus Christ, I give my allegiance.

Consider these three thoughts. Rene Descartes, that great French philosopher of the seventeenth century, made that great quote, "I think, therefore I am," Also, as one said, "For as he thinketh in his soul, so is he" (Prov 23:7). And that statement by Jesus, "I and my father are one." Dare we bring our thoughts into captivity? I think, therefore I am! Else, if not, therefore I am not. For as he thinks in his soul, so is he! If he thinks not, so is he not. Again, I and my father are one. Am I not one with my father? If not, who told thee that thou art not?

Jesus comforted his disciples with the words, "that where I am, ye may be also" (John 14:3). Notice he did not say where I go, but rather, "where I am," his present state of being. His presence expressed inwardly in that of humanity. Emmanuel—God with us. Consider the words of Pontius Pilate, "Behold the man" (John 19:5)! Both Caiaphas and Pilate characterized the

---

1. Petrelli, *Ecce Homo*, 262–265

religious and political systems of their day. And they crucified God. The Latin words used in the Vulgate translation, "Ecce Homo." Still more fitting, Behold, the God Man! Dare we ask, is he still Emmanuel? Is he still with us? "Every spirit that confesseth that Jesus Christ is come in the flesh is of God" (John 4:2). Dare we confess, he *is come* into our very own humanity today? The divine unveiling inside us, extending himself, continuing to connect with his creation. I suggest if we make ourselves comfortable and at home only and entirely in the things of the outward, we are absent from the very presence of the Lord, and not truly at home in the Spirit.

I must confess, this realization of the divine nature, this inner mystical man, this image of the divine Logos, this higher–self, is integral to the being of God, to the very divine matrix of which I write, and to the very connect-edness of all of humanity. This is the demarcation of where humanity and divinity meet, Christ the original matrix.

Are there two selves in man? Two natures, one human and one divine? Where is the division? Dare we divide and separate? "A double–minded man is unstable in all his ways" (Jas 1:8). A "two–souled" man is the original text. Yet not two distinct souls, but rather a higher and lower–self. Wavering in and out between the two, unstable and not firmly established. Still not two separate individualities. We have certainly proved that we can be alienated from God in our minds, both in word and outward practice. That does not deny the fact that we are his children, and the identity of our true authentic self, created in his image and being made (in mystical union) with his likeness, connected with the original matrix.

The humanity of the divine continues his incarnation, born in the manger of our soul. This is not to deny our human personality, nor is it to deny the being of God either. This is rather to align our understanding with the words of Jesus, "that they may be one, even as we are one" (John 17:22). There is no question that Jesus possessed a human consciousness, and it was therefore limited to a degree. For example, he was not omniscient, he only knew what the Father would have him to know, that is evident in scripture. He was Emmanuel, because of his expression of love and an out–poured life. He was the incarnation, not because he was more *God than man*, or *God and man*, but *God in man*. And again, that is not restricted to Jesus alone, as we read John, "Behold, the tabernacle of God is with men, and he will dwell with them, and they shall be his people, and God himself shall be with them, and be their God" (Rev 21:3).

It is the ever-present Christ that becomes our faith, not the historic Christ after the flesh. It is this indwelling Christ who is the "true light, which lighteth every man that cometh into the world" (John 1:9). I emphatically state that the idea of the eternal divine Logos residing in every human life does not dismiss the notion of requiring the saviourhood of Jesus Christ. It only strengthens the fact, as the mystical Christ of faith is esteemed because the Jesus of history gave him expression in a soul and body. Do not overlook that our sojourn is rooted and grounded in the chain of events of his incarnation, death, resurrection, and ascension.

8

The Doctrine of Hell

THE HOLOCAUST WAS THE genocide of Jews across Europe during World War II. My grandfather David Thomas Carroll was a flight officer killed in that terrible war. I have read that between 1941 and 1945, Nazi Germany and other allies (Axis Powers) exterminated over six million or two-thirds of the Jewish population across the continent of Europe.

Numerous methods of barbarism were conducted on human life, to man who is made in the image of God. They used gas chambers for large scale murdering of men, women, and children. Prior to unconsciousness and even suffocation (due to lack of oxygen in lungs), the condemned often convulsed and foamed at the mouth, along with vomiting, urinating, and defecating.

Then of course, there were the mass shootings, often performed by special task forces. The victims were often undressed and were placed along–side a ditch prior to their execution. It is said that some were ordered to lay down in the ditch on other dead bodies and waited for their turn to be shot. There was also extermination through labor where inmates in the concentration camps were forced to carry heavy rocks up and down stairs. With little food and weakened fragile bodies, they could not sustain this for long.

Such ethnic cleansing is viewed sinister and diabolic, and rightfully so. My wife had an aunt that recently passed, with camp numbers engraved on her arm, having been an imprisoned Jew herself. In fact, she (age 14 or thereabouts) was pulled out of an execution line (gas chamber or other, I know not) by a guard because he said she looked like his daughter. No human should bear such torture, nor witness such monstrous acts. I ask, what was the fate of the tortured Jew? Dare we think they are forever doomed in a place that far surpasses the hell they experienced while here on earth? Are we to believe their existence after death is a continuation of their prior agony, for all of eternity? Have we become so religious to not ask the right questions and challenge our long–held traditions? I appeal to the reader's conscience for an honest response.

Again, dare we condemn them to a torture chamber or condition of torment for all of eternity? If so, based on what terms? Understanding of the scripture? What if it has been wrong, our understanding? Think about it, a people that has been taught from childhood in how their promised Messiah was to appear and usher in the kingdom of heaven, a tradition that had blinded them of their long–awaited hope, that they did not accept the historical fact of two thousand years ago. So, what of their fate? Are these same men, women and children without hope? Are they further condemned to the infernal flames of hell, where there is weeping, and gnashing of teeth, and the worm dies not? Are their cries now a thousand times worse than the slaughtering of them less than a hundred years ago under a wicked Nazi regime?

I have been accused of not following the teaching of the Bible when it comes to this topic of hell, of being in the minority rather than the majority, even "warned twice," whatever that meant? My first response is pigeons flock together while eagles soar alone. My second is to come let us reason together and pray that the spirit would guide us into all truth.

One common teaching of our day is called eternal conscious torment (ECT). This doctrine has been quite popular for over fifteen hundred years, though it was not the prevailing thought in early Christianity. Gladly, more and more are learning the truth and coming out of the dark ages, along with its traditions and doctrine. Basically, ECT is the eternal torment of a person's soul for not adhering to whatever requirements a religious group puts upon salvation. The degree of their torment and the descriptions of their punishment are no less severe than that of the holocaust. Such is the doctrine of ECT or as some call it, "infernalism."

Another teaching is annihilation, which I consider the handmaiden of ECT and an equal travesty. This doctrine has gained traction of late under the banner of "conditional immortality." It basically embraces the idea that a human soul is not immortal unless it is given eternal life. Those that are non–believers will not be given immortality and therefore eventually cease to exist. They will simply perish or be destroyed once and for all, their consciousness extinguished rather than subjected to eternal suffering and torment. This is supposedly a softer approach than ECT, but if one thinks through its implications, it is equally devilish.

Now one must ask, if either of these two doctrines were remotely true, wouldn't God have warned man at the beginning of creation in the clearest of terms? Such fates exceed all the atrocities of all wars that ever were and ever shall be. Yet, God did not warn man, not even a peep! Scripture states, "But of the tree of the knowledge of good and evil, thou shalt not eat of it; for in the day that thou eatest thereof thou shalt surely die" (Gen 2:17). I can hear the objection by some, "but God meant thou shalt surely be eternally tormented or cease to exist." Why such definite and eternal consequences, yet so unclear and obscure in biblical language? No, it is rather quite clear as the record states, "in the day that thou eatest thereof thou shalt surely die." The consequence to their action was death.

Men have come to believe in the existence and continuance of human personality beyond physical death. We find in the book of Job these following words, "If a man die, shall he live" (Job 14:14)? Whether the Jews, Greeks, Persians, Egyptians, Babylonians or another ancient culture, history proves they had an interest and some form of religious thought of the hereafter.

Considering two ancient races, the Jews and the Greeks, R.J. Campbell stated, "There was considerable similarity between Hebrew and Hellenic ideas of the hereafter at an early stage in their religious history respectively, as indeed there was between them and most of their neighbors,—say from the ninth century BC to the fourth. Both assumed that the death of a human being did not involve his entire annihilation but only a drastic diminution of his hold on life. It was held that at death but little of a man survived, a dim consciousness of existing, and that this passed into a nether sphere, a region of gloom and impoverishment of most that renders life desirable. *Hades* was the Greek name for this abode, Israel called it *Sheol*. Properly speaking the name Hades pertained to the supposed superhuman ruler of the underworld but was used as a synonym for the joyless shadowland itself. Sheol on the other hand, was regarded on occasion as a synonym for the grave . . ."[1]

In the origin of the doctrine of hell, we can see certain thoughts develop in Jewish and Greco literature and custom. Later in history, especially with the conquest of Alexander the Great, more influences began to merge and blend between these two cultures. My research indicates that "sheol" is used sixty–five times in the Old Testament, with it translated into the following English words of "grave" thirty–one times, "hell" thirty–one times and "pit"

---

1. Campbell, *The Life of the World to Come*, 10–11

three times, as found in the KJV translation of the Bible. The Septuagint (Hebrew translated into Greek), used hades sixty times for sheol. Close examination of both sheol and hades demonstrates they most often, if not always, had the same meaning, namely abode, state, place or realm of the dead.

In fact, the word "hades" comes from the Greek word *a(i)des* and means un–perceive, unknown, imperceptible or unseen. The English word hell comes from the Anglo–Saxon word *helan* or *hillan* meaning cavern, denoting concealed or unseen place. It was not inappropriate to say, "I plan to hell my potatoes" or "a young couple sought hell for a kiss."

I find it quite interesting that we find the word sheol only used four times in the entire book of Genesis. We find Jacob stating that he would go down into hell mourning the supposed death of his son Joseph (Gen 37:35). Likewise, three additional times in this book we find the faithful mentioning sheol as the place they go upon their death. Furthermore, in scanning other verses in the Old Testament, it is apparent that they understood there was a joining or "gathering unto their fathers" in the unseen world. In other words, in the first two thousand years of human history, according to scripture, it appears that afterlife was not a frequent or dominating topic; however I would suggest that other evidence indicates there was still interest, including the pursuit by some to converse with the departed.

It has been noted by another that the great theologian C.S. Lewis in his book Reflections on the Psalms stated, "It seem quite clear that in most parts of the Old Testament there is little or no belief in the future life, certainly no belief that is of any religious importance." R.J. Campbell offers further insight by having said, "The remark is often made that Old Testament religion has no belief in personal survival after death, but this would be an erroneous deduction from the comparative silence of the scriptures on the subject, as we have observed.

"There was sufficient reason for the silence, but it did not correspond to current belief and practice. On the contrary there is plenty of proof that the Jew was like his neighbors in endeavouring to establish communication with the departed whom he continued to think of, not as dead, but as in some sense still alive and interested in the good or evil lot of those remaining on earth. We have only to recall the story of Saul and the witch of Endor with its account of the converse of the troubled king with the shade of the prophet Samuel to be sure of this and the inference that the incident was not singular."[2]

I would add, near silence of the scripture does not suggest there was no belief in existence in the beyond. On the contrary, it was assumed. It is

2. Campbell, *The Life of the World to Come,* 39

sufficient to say that in the development and progression of early Jewish thought, the primary focus was more on the existence of here and now, and less on the hereafter.

In earlier times, death was more dreaded than welcomed, separating a person from the happiness of life. It was not considered a hopeful step into immorality but rather one of disappointment and loss. Only a few were considered victors, like Enoch or Elijah for the Jew and Hercules for the Greek.

When reading scriptures during certain periods in time, we can sense the Jewish apprehension of the afterlife. As stated by Hezekiah, "For the grave (sheol) cannot praise thee, death cannot celebrate thee: they that go down into the pit cannot hope for thy truth" (Isa 38:18). It is a grave error to think that people in the Old Testament thought of 'non–existence' in the hereafter. Annihilation advocates miss this point entirely. The Jewish mind thought of fullness of life in the here and now while the hereafter was considered something less, outside the interest, care and divine purposes of God. In fact, here is what they thought at one time, "The dead praise not the Lord, neither any that go down into silence" (Ps. 115:17). When you read verses as these, you must put them into their culture and time period rather than cementing a doctrine of it.

In consideration of the lack of support of eternal conscience torment in the Old Testament, that brilliant scholar of the nineteenth century, Thomas Baldwin Thayer wrote the following, "We may, therefore, expect to find it announced in plainest language at the very beginning—certainly on those occasions of sin and crime which could not fail to call out some declaration of it, some threat or warning in regard to it. But not a word do we hear of it on any such occasion. The first transgression, Cain, the Deluge, the destruction of Sodom and Gomorrah, are all passed without a single line in the sacred record respecting it. The just inference is that it cannot be true, or God would certainly have said something about it, in the course of the two thousand five hundred years of the Patriarchal Period.

"We next examined the Law of Moses, the entire catalogue of its penalties and threatenings; but in no case did we find the least allusion to the doctrine of endless punishments, or any punishments or rewards beyond death. And we showed by the acknowledgements of the most learned critics and theologians, themselves believers in the doctrine, that it was not taught in the Law of Moses, but that the Old Testament dispensation was wholly a dispensation of temporal rewards and punishments."[3]

I find it incredibly interesting that there was no communication of such an idea from God to his creation, no warning in the least bit. Certainly,

---

3. Thayer, *The Origin and History of the Doctrine of Endless Punishment,* 115–116

a hint or bread crumb, if indeed such a fate were in store for them. Shouldn't justice demand it? Wouldn't love cry in the streets for it? Yet, four thousand years of silence without instruction or clarity of such dreadful consequences? Still, other nations and religions had afterlife ideas of eternal rewards and punishments, but not God's own people, his chosen? To the Jew, there was no distinction of rewards and punishments for life beyond. We find in scripture, "All things come alike to all, there is one event to the righteous, and to the wicked; to the good and to the clean, and to the unclean; to him that sacrificeth and to him that sacrificeth not: as is the good, so is the sinner; and he that sweareth, as he that feareth an oath" (Ecc 9:2).

Fast forwarding in history, the idea of having no distinction between the good and the bad in the hereafter would not last for long. This is where the Greek mind began to make more of rewards for those supposedly more deserving, while the Jew gave more attention to the idea and hope of the resurrection of the body. Again, R.J. Campbell said, "The idea of the resurrection had no charm for the Greek mind, and that of a bodiless form of personal existence was inconceivable to the Jew."[4]

I would be remiss to not mention that there were sporadic comments here and there in the Old Testament indicating a more positive view of the afterlife experience than the common belief of most Jews. For example, we find, "God will redeem my soul from the power of the sheol; for he shall receive me" (Ps 49:15). In summary, the Jewish mind understood their allegiance to One God and looked forward to the establishment of the kingdom on earth, with their nation set as God's favored. This was their focus, with resurrection playing a role in the return of their fathers.

By the time we get to the New Testament, certain thoughts toward the afterlife had developed among people. The Jews adopted the heathen teaching of eternal punishment in the afterlife. Since they did not learn of it from their own scriptures, scholars have come to understand various ideas of neighboring nations were adopted by the Jews during the time period interval between the Old and New Testament, commonly known as the silent years of prophecy. In departing from their law and commandments of God and endorsing other religious fables as new traditions, Jesus rebukes them, "Making the word of God of none effect through your traditions . . ." (Mark 7:3).

Again, that excellent scholar Thayer wrote of the origin of endless punishment, "At the close of the Old Testament scriptures they did not believe it; at the beginning of the New they did. Between these two points of time there was an interval of some four hundred years, during which there was

4. Campbell, *The Life of the World to Come*, 43

no prophet in Israel. Malachi was the last of the Hebrew prophets, and from him to Christ there stretches this waste period of four centuries, when the Jews were without any divine teacher or revelation from heaven. And all this while they were in constant and close intercourse with the heathen, especially the Egyptians, the Greeks and Romans, who held the doctrine in review as part of the national faith. From these, therefore, they must have borrowed it, for it is certain that they could not have obtained it from any inspired source, since none was open to them during this period."[5]

During the times of the Old Testament, it is quite apparent that they were limited in their understanding of life beyond the grave. The prophets and psalmists of old never really had more than partial glimpses of afterlife. Yet, we are expressly told that Christ brought life and immorality to light: meaning not only a much clearer understanding, but those of yesteryear were in darkness to a large degree.

In reading the New Testament, the Greek word *hades* is used eleven times, with it translated *hell* ten times and *grave* once. The Greek word *gehenna* is used twelve times, each translated into our English word *hell*, and the Greek word *tartarus* is used once, again as *hell*. I have heard it said that Jesus spoke more about hell than any other topic in the scripture. Not remotely true. He used hades approximately five times (one was repeated in another gospel) plus gehenna an estimated eleven times (several repeats). Therefore, he mentioned hell about twelve or thirteen times in total. Yet a quick scan of the use of heaven in the gospels exceeds one hundred times, most of them used by Jesus Christ.

As mentioned earlier, hades meaning the abode, state, place or realm of the dead. It meant basically the same as sheol in the Old Testament. Another later development of hades was the different sections or compartments, one for the good and another for the bad, both separated by a river or great gulf. The good section in hell was considered paradise. When Jesus retold the former Jewish parable of the rich man and Lazarus, this idea of compartments was included in the story. Albeit, it does not mean Jesus himself believed in sections of hell, not any more than when he spoke of the Philistine god of filth, Beelzebub. His audience understood the stories and their meaning, while our time struggles to grasp the significance.

We can see hades was used in a figurative sense too. Jesus said, "And thou Capernaum, which is exalted unto heaven, shalt be brought down to hell (hades): for if the mighty works, which have been done in thee, had been done in Sodom, it would have remained until this day" (Matt 11:23). In Luke's gospel we find, Capernaum will be thrust down. This speaks of a

---

5. Thayer, *The Origin and History of the Doctrine of Endless Punishment*, 98–99

state of woe, utter ruin or desolation. It is said in another place that the soul of Jesus was not left in hell because of his resurrection. Even Paul, although only using once the word hell, said of hades, "O death, where is thy sting? O hades, where is thy victory" (1 Cor 15:55)? Everyone in hades will not be left there but rather delivered up (Rev 20:13)! Why there are many that insist that hell will not release its captives, I shall never understand.

I will make a rather bold statement, perhaps to the shock of some. As a Christian, I may find it necessary to be in hell in the afterlife. Why would I dare say such a thing? If Jesus is the same yesterday, today and forever, then his unending love to redeem will never be satisfied until he rescues the very last soul from hades. And if we are to follow the Lamb wherever he is to go, then we find ourselves with him in hades too, to be with him. But let us first learn and rescue those that are in hell while on earth. For this reason, I believe hades is a realm or dimension of consciousness and existence that is far more than any place, it is a state or condition of the soul, whether in the here and now, as well as in the hereafter.

Then, we have the word Gehenna, which is the Greek form of Gee Hinnom, a Hebrew word meaning the Valley of Hinnom. This was a valley just south in Jerusalem. Jeremiah says, "For the children of Judah have done evil in my sight, saith the Lord: they have set their abominations in the house called by my name, to pollute it. And they built the high places of Tophet, which is in the valley of Hinnom, to burn their sons and daughters in the fire, which I commanded them not, neither came it into my heart" (Jer 7:30–31). Gehenna was a place where they once sacrificed children. Scholars have come to understand that drums were beaten to drown out the cries of the victims. After captivity, Jews regarded this place as one of abhorrence on account of abomination. They continued to throw dead bodies of criminals and animals there. Moreso, to prevent pestilence, constant perpetual fires were maintained to consume what was dumped there. In the New Testament, we find that Jesus Christ used the word Gehenna as a figurative or symbolic meaning of judgment. That is why we have proportional degrees of offense followed by equal degrees of judgment in Matthew or when James compares the tongue and its conversation of filthiness compared to the setting of fire in the dumps of Gehenna. It would be incorrect to suggest he used the word to mean an eternal torture chamber in the afterlife.

Much more could and has been said on this subject of hell. In God's divine matrix, all hell is eradicated by the very presence of his Christ. It is for this reason that we preach the restoration of all of humanity and reject eternal conscious torment and annihilation, with Christ victorious over all of creation.

9

Ninety-Five Theses

Here are brief explanations defending the ultimate reconciliation of God towards all men, while protesting opposing views. If per chance the first ninety-four do not convince you, I believe the last may be quite compelling. I pray that my objection is with a spirit of humility, kindness, and compassion, yet direct when necessary. I believe in the ultimate end of all sin and consequent holiness and happiness for all of humanity.

1. "If the mighty works which were done in you had been done in Tyre and Sidon, they would have repented long ago in sackcloth and ashes" (Matt 11:20–24). Nineteenth-Century English Theologian Samuel Cox wrote, "The Lord himself declared that even the guilty inhabitants of Sodom and Tyre would have been brought to repentance and life had they witnessed the mighty works wrought in the favoured cities of Galilee! Why were they not permitted to witness them, then? Can we blame them, and condemn them to an eternal death or an eternal misery, because they did not see what they could not see, because they did not repent, when the very means which would infallibly have induced repentance were not vouchsafed them?"[1]

---

1. Cox, *Salvator Mundi: Or, Is Christ The Saviour of All Men?*, 1–2

2. Again, Samuel Cox said of Jesus, "He was quite sure that if they (miracles) had been done in Sodom, and Tyre, and Sidon, these great cities would have repented and remained," and "He claims to know that the men of Sodom and of Tyre and Sidon would not have resisted the influences which failed to bring the men of Galilee to repentance and life."[2]

3. Considering those that lived in Tyre and Sidon, reason and conscience demands that if God chose to not bring them to repentance, their opportunity to have eternal life should not be limited to the time they had lived compared to two thousand years later and therefore repenting, had they seen the mighty works of Christ.

4. It does not seem reasonable that a God of perfect love, goodness and justice should subject a person to a correction "without end," and certainly not to any type of torture in the least. In fact, the very suggestion of endless penalties contradicts the purpose and true end of correction.

5. The love of the father in the story of the prodigal son is an exact picture of the love of our heavenly father towards his lost children.

6. "Also unto thee, O LORD, belongeth mercy; for thou renderest to every man according to his work" (Ps 62:12). Here God gives to man out of his mercy, although those that oppose us would have us to believe he renderest to every man out of this justice, withholding mercy.

7. "For therefore we both labour and suffer reproach, because we trust in the living God, who is the Saviour of all men, specially of those that believe. These things command and teach" (I Tim 4:10–11). I do not apologize for rubbing against common teachings of our day, for we are called to command and teach that Christ is the Saviour of not only a few, nor only a special elect, but rather of all men. Christ is the answer for all of humanity!

8. Now, don't you find it somewhat interesting that Paul would add the words "especially of those believing." It means most of all, especially, particularly, in a greater degree or chiefly. The word "especially" comes from a Greek word *malista*, which means most of all, or particularly. In other words, we are to know that for those who believe, the Lord Jesus is most of all, or in-particular our savior. From an experiential standpoint, Jesus has become their salvation.

---

2. Cox, *Salvator Mundi: Or, Is Christ The Saviour of All Men?*, 13–14.

9. Paul connects the idea of salvation and all men by having stated, "I exhort therefore, that, first of all, supplications, prayers, intercessions, and giving of thanks, be made for all men; For kings and for all that are in authority; that we may lead a quiet and peaceable life in all godliness and honesty. For this is good and acceptable in the sight of God our Saviour; who will have all men to be saved, and to come unto the knowledge of the truth . . . Who gave himself a ransom for all, to be testified in due time" (I Tim 2:1–6). This is not simply a flimsy "wish" as some would imagine, for God needs not to wish as a child would "wish upon a star" or "make a birthday wish."

10. The original word "will" is *thelo*, and has the meaning of—as being inclined, determined, choosing, preferring, desire, to be about to, to delight in or to be willing. Job supports our argument by having said, "and what his soul desireth, even that he doeth." (Job 23:13) Paul clearly informs us that God wills the salvation of all men.

11. We are to pray for the salvation of all men. And if we do not think God desires to save all, why would we pray against his will?

12. To make the claim to be the ransom for all and yet redeem only a few is a contradiction of terms and absurd. He will have all to be testified in due time.

13. Again, Paul provides us with the statement, "For as in Adam all die, even so in Christ shall all be made alive. But every man in his own order" (1 Cor 15:22–23). Another translation states "For even as, in Adam, all are dying, thus also, in Christ, shall all be vivified. Yet each in his own class." It is evident that each, as a result of being in Adam, have all experienced that state of death, from cradle to grave. And as *all* have tasted of this death, so shall this *same all* be made alive. To suggest the *second all* is somehow restricted completely ignores the structure of the sentence. All who endured the first shall enjoy the second.

14. What does it mean to be "made alive?" We first must understand what it means for all to die. God told Adam "And dying, you shall die," there would be a process of dying, coupled with a condition of death, resulting in physical death. This is the state of being of all of humanity "in Adam." Yet, we are made alive "in Christ," participating in his life.

15. Professor of Philosophy and Author Thomas Talbott recently wrote of I Corinthians 15:22 and Romans 11:32, "we encounter a contrast between two universal statements, and in each case the first 'all' determines the scope of the second." Again, he writes of verse 15:22, "The

grammatical evidence here seems utterly decisive; you can reject it only if you are prepared to reject what is right there before your eyes."[3]

16. "But every man in his own order" (1 Cor 15:23). Paul continues his thought by stating, every man in his own order. That is, all who shall be made alive in the Christ will be made alive in their own proper time, sequence, degree, position, band, rank, or group.

17. "Therefore, as by the offence of one judgment came upon all men to condemnation; even so by the righteousness of one upon all men unto justification of life" (Rom 5:18). Notice the clarity within the structure and context of the statement. The "all" that have been condemned are the same "all" unto justification of life. Suffice it to say, the text means what it says.

18. As one man (Adam) leads all of humanity into condemnation, even so one man (Jesus Christ) leads all to justification of life.

19. The triumph of Jesus Christ far exceeds the one trespass of Adam. To condemn most of humanity to eternal consciousness torment or annihilation is not a victory but rather a monumental defeat beyond imagination.

20. Why it would bother some today that God will save all is beyond me. Israel had also been concerned that God would save the Gentiles too. I see little difference between those of today and Israel of old.

21. Jesus is the same yesterday, today and forever. What makes us think that his compassion and saving ability is only limited to saving a soul while here on earth and not the afterlife? Jesus saves without limitation or hinderance of any sort or kind, physical or spiritual.

22. "For God hath concluded them all in unbelief, that he might have mercy upon all" (Rom 11:32). Again, the scope of the first "all" determines the scope of the second "all." The Concordant Literal version states, "For God locks up all together in stubbornness, that he should be merciful to all." And if he should be merciful, he who is rich in mercy, does not withhold it. This is the conclusion to "what shall we say then? Is there unrighteousness with God? God forbid" (Rom 9:14). This allows for the totality of both Jews and Gentiles to have mercy. In this, Paul wants to make known the mercy of God, by which he makes the unbelief of some the salvation for others, and vice-versa. Here we find Paul concluding that *all* are bound in unbelief and *all* receive mercy.

---

3. Talbott, *The INESCAPABLE LOVE of GOD*, 55

23. "For if through the offence of one many be dead, much more the grace of God, and the gift by grace, which is by one man, Jesus Christ, hath abounded unto many" (Rom 5:15). The distinction of the "one" and the "many" denotes singular verses plural. This is important and should not be overlooked. Within the context of the chapter, it becomes clear the plural denotes "all."

24. Of course, all does not always mean all in every single Bible verse. Language must be considered within its context and sentence structure. All may refer to the "all" at the party, or "all" within the house. Opponents to universal reconciliation make the point that "all does not mean all" and mistakenly apply this same logic to several other verses using the word "all." Let good grammar and common sense prevail when making these distinctions.

25. John stated, "And he is the propitiation for our sins: and not for ours only, but also for the whole world" (1 John 2:2). Christ is the *propitiation* for our sins, that is, he is the satisfaction, atonement, amendment, conciliation or expiation for our sins. For whom? It does not say, "for only those who believe," but rather "for the whole world."

26. "And when all things shall be subdued unto him, then shall the Son also himself be subject unto him that put all things under him, that God may be all in all" (1 Cor 15:28). The apostle Paul confirms what David said in Psalms 110:1, namely *all* enemies are made his footstool.

27. All things in the universe are to be brought into subjection to God. Certainly, if all things are subdued, then God shall be *all in all*, or everything to everyone.

28. What is that subjection with which all things are subdued that God may be all and in all? Can it be none other than 'salvation' to be subjected to Christ? Even David said "stilled (subjected) is my soul, for from him is my salvation" (Ps 62:1–2 CLV).

29. The idea of "at the name of Jesus every knee should bow, of things in heaven, and things in earth, and things under the earth. . . .to the *glory* of God the Father," denotes a *subjection* to Jesus, and of the knee of *every* person. Shall we not gladly bow the knee to his glory?

30. "And, having made peace through the blood of his cross, by him to reconcile all things unto himself; by him, I say whether they be things in earth, or things in heaven" (Col 1:20). It does not say he reconciles some things, but rather he reconciles all things.

31. To reconcile means to unite, to bring back into harmony, to make consistent or compatible. To reconcile *all* is to restore and bring *all* into new creation life.

32. "For of him, and through him, and to him, all things." (Rom 11:36) God is the source of all things, as out of him, and through him, and back to him are all things, restoring all.

33. "He that descended is the same also that ascended up far above all heavens, that he might fill all things" (Eph 4:9–10). My mentor of many years, J. Preston Eby writes, "The message is clear, redemption does not include only the salvation of mankind, as wonderful and glorious as that aspect is, but it also includes the complete transformation of the entire universe so that God shall fill all things."[4] Apart from Christ, can anything truly be filled?

34. Seventeenth–century theologian Elhanan Winchester stated, "God hath said to his Son, 'Ask of me, and I shall give thee the heathen for thine inheritance, and the uttermost parts of the earth for thy possession' (Ps 2:8). Thus, all things are given to Christ, without exception."[5]

35. God was in Christ reconciling the world unto himself (2 Cor 5:19). Is God's love and reach *limited* to the physical world? It is not!

36. He that descended is the same who ascended, that he might fill all things. He emptied himself that he may fill all.

37. Peter indicated that Christ, being put to death and quickened by the Spirit, preached to those in prison, the gospel (good news), to those that were dead, that they may live according to God in the spirit. Orthodoxy has always been clear on the descent of Christ into hades with the release of captivity.

38. Apostolic Father Ignatius had stated, "He descended, indeed, into Hades alone, but He arose accompanied by a multitude."[6]

39. Does not his cross span beyond the grave to reach the dead? Is he not the Lord of both the living and the dead? Paul made it clear that death is swallowed up in victory. The triumph of the cross will consume death wherever it may be. "O death, where is thy sting? O hades, where is thy victory" (I Cor 15:54)?

---

4. Eby, *God All in All—Saviour of the World Series*, 28

5. Winchester, *The Universal Restoration*, 186

6. Ignatius. *Epistle of Ignatius to the Trallians*, 70

40. "For if the casting away of them be the reconciling of the world, what shall the receiving of them be, but life from the dead" (Rom 11:15). This seems to indicate postmortem salvation for Israel, as many will have already passed to the other side.

41. "But now is Christ risen from the dead and become the first of them that slept" (I Cor 15:20). The word *slept* is in the past tense and clearly indicates that they are not sleeping any longer. Christ has led them from the power of death into the life of his resurrection.

42. "And I, if I be lifted up from the earth, will draw all men unto me" (John 12:32). The word for 'draw' means to drag, as to wrap up, pull, move, thrust, or to drive. Your stubborn will cannot stop his passion of love towards you, he will eventually win you over, as he will draw all men unto himself.

43. Jesus did not say he will draw a *few* or *some*, or just the elect. He emphatically said *all*.

44. John states, ". . .that the Father hath sent the Son to be the Saviour of the world" (I John 4:14). Either he saves the world, or he does not. To win a small percentage makes the gospel a complete failure for the rest of humanity.

45. Bible teachers speak of the love and mercies of God, then teach of endless punishment and ongoing torture beyond human description; penalties unfit for the worst of offenders. They proclaim *good news* for all, then follow with *bad news* for most. This is double minded at its worst.

46. In the parable of the rich man and Lazarus, whatever you think of the story and whatever you believe hades to be, we can see positive *change* in the attitude of the rich man.

47. The story of the rich man and Lazarus is one story of five in a single parable. It speaks of the Jews and Gentiles and is not a literal story, unless you think a single drop of water could in any measure alleviate the excruciating pain of a never–ending flame.

48. Likewise, in the same parable, there was a great gulf fixed in which he could not pass. However, it does not say that he could not be rescued by the One who could pass. Furthermore, this story is connected to other stories in the same parable, namely that the shepherd will leave the ninety–nine sheep to save the one that went astray.

49. The popular view of hell is that God will never love his enemies enough to save them but rather subject them to spend their entire existence in a state of godless torment and never–ending punishment because he

himself is subject to his own supposed justice. Contrary to this notion, Jesus showed us the heart of the Father when he said to love your enemies.

50. Nineteenth–century theologian Thomas Allin states, "If God's attitude towards his worst of foes is love, that attitude is permanent, is eternal; nay must be so. Whatever be the sin of his enemies, he must be to them the same unchanging God of love, and never more so than when he most inexorably punishes. Note the emphatic 'But I say unto you, love your enemies.' Here is the very heart of God disclosed; here is the dividing line; here the spiritual watershed between a true and false theology." Is God not going to love his enemies?[7]

51. For God so loved the world. Does his love ever cease, whether here on earth or the afterlife? Does a parent ever stop loving their child? Would a loving parent ever turn their back on their child if they are crying and begging for mercy? God's paternal love for humanity far surpasses our expectations.

52. Jesus said to love your enemies and do good. This is what Christ himself would have us to do. Israel desired vengeance on their enemies. Is God more like Israel or like Jesus? Is God to turn his back on the enemies of the cross or is he to love them and do good? Jesus came to reveal the Father, so what did he say again? The Father has forgiven and loves those opposed to him.

53. Has God become the great taskmaster of Egypt, dividing, or placing a schism into the very Being of God, representing him as the unchanging God of love to a wrathful just God of the hereafter for most of his creation? This dualism simply will not do.

54. The book of Revelation informs us that God shall wipe away all tears from their eyes; and there shall be no more death, sorrow, pain and crying. Consider a loving mother or father in heaven with a lost son in eternal conscious torment or having been annihilated. Who honestly believes they would not remember their son and continue to shed tears? Some have suggested we would be so immersed into worshipping the Lord, we will not have time to think of our lost loved ones. Nonsense!

55. "Gracious is the LORD, and righteous; yea, our God is merciful" (Psalms 116:5). Saint Basil the Great (330 AD—379 AD) referred to

---

7. Allin, *Christ Triumphant*, 48–49

this verse that everywhere scripture connects God's justice (righteousness) with his compassions.

56. There is not opposition between mercy and justice, as if justice is punishment of sin without the slightest hint of mercy, nor is mercy forgiveness of sin without the least indication of correction. This false belief makes a schism to the very character and nature of God. He is not *just* without *mercy*, nor is he merciful without righteousness.

57. We think of words like *eternal* and *everlasting* as unending, perpetual, surpassing all time and space. However, this is not how they were used by the early Christians. They rather, most often, carried the meaning of a duration of time having a specific purpose and therefore end. The Greek word is *aion*, from which we have translated into English as *eon*. The word denotes a period-of-time, and often are translated as an *age*. He is the God of the ages, or age and ages.

58. Jonah was afflicted in the belly of the great fish (note: Fenton indicated this was a name for a ship)[8], and said, "her bars was about me forever," (Hebrew is *owlam*, which is same as *aion*). The story tells us that he was in the belly for three days and nights, a specific time-period of "forever." Was then Jonah three days in the belly of hell "eternal" and "everlasting" as we may often think of the meaning? No, his period-of-time was three days, or forever.

59. If forever meant unending, there would be no reason to say forever and ever (e.g., times, times, and times and a half).

60. We find several references of the Aaronic priesthood as an *everlasting* priesthood (Ex 40:15), yet the New Testament tells us it ended (Heb 7:12), since a better covenant and more excellent ministry was established. Simply, the word denotes a duration of time that had ended.

61. The eternal (*qedem*) God is thy refuge means antiquity, just as the ancient (*qedem*) mountains are found in scripture. It is better stated, "The God of the ages is thy refuge." This is what is meant in holy script that God is eternal. Yet we certainly understand he is also perpetual and without beginning or end.

62. He has given us an incorruptible life and this life can not be corrupted, degraded, nor end. In the time and space continuum, we live this life through the ages. This is eternal life, or the life of the ages. This is that which Jesus spoke, "I am come that they might have life, and that they might have it more abundantly." (John 10:10) That is, to have this life

---

8. Fenton, *The Holy Bible in Modern English*, 624

be superabundant and have its preeminence in our soul. Note: When we speak of eternal (*aionios*) life and everlasting (*aionios*) punishment, one must keep in mind that *aionios* is an adjective and is there to support their nouns.

63. The concept of everlasting punishment is age–abiding correction in the original Greek. Once correction serves its purpose, it ends.

64. Nineteenth–century theologian Thomas Baldwin Thayer writes, "He (Paul) is entirely silent in regard to the wicked in the resurrection; and either there are no wicked when the 'end' comes, or they are not raised. He speaks of those who are Christ's, but makes not the least allusion to those who are not his; and the legitimate inference is, that there are none of this sort, but that all are Christ's, and Christ is God's; and he, as the Father, is all in all."[9]

65. God is a consuming fire, and there will be those that have their part in the purging and cleansing judgment of God symbolized as the lake of fire. The fire is to consume the dross but not the gold and silver, the chaff but not the wheat, burning away that which is not pure and unworthy of his kingdom. I think many have passed (or are passing through) this phase of their spiritual journey, in this life and beyond.

66. Paul wrote in I Corinthians chapter three that if any man's work shall be burned, he shall suffer loss: but he himself shall be saved; yet so as by fire.

67. The book of Revelation states, "And death and hell were cast into the lake of fire" (Rev 20:14). Even death and hell shall be consumed, removed, destroyed, and abolished.

68. "Behold, I make all things new" (Rev 21:5). When God says he makes *all* things new, it does not mean some things, or only things in heaven, but rather *all* things. Imagine that, he makes all things new. Note: It also begs the question and consideration of the idea of "non-things."

69. After the lake of fire, have you ever noticed that Jesus continues to bid them to come? "And the Spirit and the bride say, Come. And let him that heareth say, Come. And let him that is athrist come. And whosoever will, let him take the water of life freely" (Rev 22:17). Praise the Lord, no longer in bondage but liberated and wanting to drink of the water of his life, as would anyone who might have been through a fire.

---

9. Thayer, *Theology of Universalism*, 225

70. "All flesh shall see the salvation of God," according to Luke 3:6. What are we to make of this verse? Luke is quoting from Isaiah chapter forty in this passage. This points to a salvation which is universal in scope.

71. Jesus came to save that which was lost. Will he really do what he has come to do? Can we trust him at his word? Shall he be a failure and save only a few? If multitudes of souls are lost, whether to eternal torment or cease to exist, then they are not rescued by Jesus, and he failed his mission.

72. It is a known fact and well documented that many early fathers of the church embraced universal reconciliation or the restoration of all humanity. Reading the fathers will convince a person of this truth. Examples include, but not limited to: Origen without hesitation called eternal fire to be finite, Jerome calling the flame of Gehenna purifying, and Greggory of Nyssa taught the same of eternal fire.

73. It is my present understanding that an outer darkness with great sorrow, weeping and gnashing of teeth will be experienced for those that deny the Lord, yet after the "uttermost farthing" is paid, salvation will come to them. It will cost them their lower soul life with all of its selfish vices.

74. Nineteenth-century theologian Hosea Ballou stated, "It is unreasonable to allow that divine justice can require any punishment or retribution which divine love does not desire."[10]

75. It is not uncommon to find many Christians desiring salvation and thinking of it as "fire insurance" and escape from a supposed place of fire and torture. This desire is driven by fear, whereas universal reconciliation is driven by the goodness of God towards all men, and we as living epistles proclaim "be ye reconciled."

76. Peter had said, "Whom the heaven must receive until the times of restitution of all things" (Acts 3:21). The Wuest translation reads, "times when all things will be restored to their pristine glory," and Phillips reads, "that universal restoration of which God spoke in ancient times . . ." Are we to believe in the restitution of all, or only in the restitution of the elect?

77. Paul states, "That in the dispensation of the fulness of times he might gather together in one all things in Christ, both which are in heaven, and which are in earth; in him" (Eph 1:10). When the times had run

10. Ballou, *A Voice to Universalists*, 26

their course to the end or reached their fulfillment, God will gather together in one all things in the Christ, under Christ, or unto Christ.

78. The last enemy to be destroyed is death. Therefore, we can conclude that death is once and for all destroyed. As one has so wisely said, "Death has an expiration date."

79. Many are taught there are no second chances on the other side. Your decision here determines your eternal fate. Sound familiar? Then they concoct an "age of accountability" theory, that if you are young enough, and die before a certain age, you will have another chance to choose in the afterlife. So, which is it? Of course, it is fortunate for the child that dies before reaching accountability, and unfortunate if after that day. The fallacy of such an assertion boggles the mind.

80. Narrow is the way that leads to life, and few there be that will find it. Christ came to give us more abundant life, this quality of life in the here and now. Indeed, it is rare for a person to seek it out and find it, the true reality of it. However, when reading verses about wide is the gate and broad is the way that leadeth to destruction and strait is the gate and narrow the way that leads to life, the idea of heaven and hell is simply not in the context, nor should it be inserted there. Make no mistake, God has set before us the way of life and the way of death; in the path of righteousness is life, but the way of error leads to death.

81. The nineteenth-Cambridge scholar Andrew Jukes wrote of those that have accepted the view of annihilation, "though a great step in advance of the doctrine of endless woe, it is not a perfect witness of the mind of God, nor the true solution of the great mystery. God has not made man to let him fall almost as soon as made, and then, in a large proportion of his seed, to sin yet more, and suffer, and be annihilated; but rather out of and through the fall to raise him even to higher and more secure blessedness, as it is written, 'As in Adam all die, so in Christ shall all be made alive.'"[11] I think that the suggestion of suffering of fewer or more stripes, according to their measure of transgression, to then be eternally annihilated (e.g., no longer to exist) by the second death is as devilish a thought as is eternal consciousness torment.

82. Then there is the parable of the sheep and the goats in Matthew chapter 25. The one goes into life eternal and the other into everlasting punishment. The entire story is rich with meaning, as Jesus informs us of our treatment of others is a direct treatment towards himself. So, by their actions, one reaps age–abiding life and the other age–enduring

11. Jukes, *Restitution of All Things*, 84

correction. Yet, once correction has served its purpose, salvation comes to the all, including the goats in this case.

83. Jesus tells us that the gates of hell shall not prevail against his church. Jesus has the keys to death and hell, and there is no gate that shall keep Christ and his host of overcomers from storming those gates and leading captivity free. Likewise, there is no gate that can keep creation bound for all of eternity.

84. Author, teacher and practicing attorney Richard Murray writes, "When people refer me to consider with fear the impenetrable gates of a tortuous hell, I counter by referring them to consider with awe the indefatigable arms of a rescuing savior."[12]

85. Again, Richard Murray stated, "I remember the Jubilee day of my own personal discovery that God was not an eternal torturer but a relentless rescuer. I literally slapped my forehead and said, 'How could I miss that?' So many in the fresh and fearless early church would not allow satanic attributes to be attributed to a Father God. They instantly and intuitively knew that inflicting eternal conscious torment on his children was irreconcilable with a loving Abba. And they readily barred and exiled it from their theology. Unlike us, the early church didn't have 1,500 years of indoctrinated cement from which to blast out. Thank God Jesus has kept his powder dry and potent for us to use as needed for such a day as this."[13]

86. And again, Richard Murray writes, "'Like water spilled on the ground, which cannot be recovered, so must we die. But that is not what God desires; rather, he devises ways so that a banished person *does not remain banished* from him' (II Sam 14:14). Amazing verse. It reveals God's will is that we not die or suffer banishment. He is perpetually *devising* ways for us to recognize and realize His restorative power. This is the essential heart of the 'good shepherd' which leaves the flock of ninety–nine to rescue and restore one lost sheep . . . 'So, why would we *ever* limit God's ability to rescue exiles *only* on *this* side of death? Restoration of those in exile is an essential quality of the divine nature. Some claim Hell to be the 'ultimate exile', so why would God not perpetually devise ways for the 'ultimate restoration?' . . . Are we so cocksure that God cannot *ever* 'devise a way' for the postmortem exile. Who are we to do so limiting the reconciling power of God."[14]

12. Murray, *Facebook post*
13. Murray, *Facebook post*
14. Murray, *Facebook post*

87. Hans Urs Von Balthasar was considered by the Pope as perhaps the greatest scholar that the Catholic church had ever had in its history. He died days before having been ordained a Cardinal of the church. He wrote a book titled "Dare we hope that all men be saved." He could not say with certainty, but he did hope it be true, and would insist on knowing nothing that would deny it not to be true.[15]

88. Eastern Orthodox scholar of religion and philosopher, David Bentley Hart, writes of two questions that must be answered: first whether the God who creates a reality in which the eternal suffering of any being is possible, even if it should be a self–induced suffering, can in fact be the infinitely good God of love that Christianity says he is; and second question of whether this defiant rejection of God for all of eternity is really logically possible for any rational being.[16]

89. Early church father Origen stated, "We believe, however, that the goodness of God through Christ will restore his entire creation to one end, even his enemies, being conquered and subdued."[17]

90. One of the most respected and loved fathers of the Christian church was Gregory of Nyssa (fourth century). It is well documented that he was a defender of the salvation of all men.

91. Saint Augustine himself admitted, "those tender–hearted Christians who decline to believe that any, or that all of those whom the infallibly just Judge may pronounce worthy of the punishment of hell, shall suffer eternally, and who suppose that they shall be delivered after a fixed term of punishment, longer or shorter according to the amount of each man's sin."[18] David Bently Hart wrote that Augustine referred to such persons as "the merciful–hearted." Furthermore, Thomas Talbott wrote of Augustine stating in the Enchiridion, "It is quite in vain, then, that some—indeed very many—yield to merely human feelings and deplore the notion of the eternal punishment of the damned and their interminable and perpetual misery."[19]

92. Theologian and author Peter Hiett wrote, "Then I looked and I heard around the throne and the living creatures and the elders the voice of many angels, numbering myriads of myriads and thousands of thousands, saying with a loud voice, 'Worthy is the Lamb who was slain,

15. Balthasar, *Dare We Hope That All Men Be Saved?*, 18

16. Hart, *THAT ALL shall be SAVED*, 17

17. Origen, *On First Principles*, 70

18. Augustine, *The City of God*, 939

19. Talbott, *The INESCAPABLE LOVE of GOD*, 16

to receive power and wealth and wisdom and might and honor and glory and blessing!' And I heard every creature in heaven and earth and under the earth and in the sea, and all that is in them, saying, 'To him who sits on the throne and to the Lamb be blessing and honor and glory and might forever and ever!' And the four living creatures said, 'Amen!' and the elders fell down and worshipped." I have wondered if this 'all' might only be the 'all' alive at the time, however this hardly fits the context of the opening of the seven-sealed scroll. And furthermore, they praise the lamb that was slain and join the elders who praise the lamb because he 'ransomed people for God' (v.9)."[20]

93. For creation itself shall be delivered from the bondage of corruption into the glorious liberty of the children of God. This is total liberation extended to all of creation, as heaven invades earth. Reconciliation is not for humanity alone, but for the whole creation.

94. Isaiah tells us in chapter forty–five that God says to look unto him to be saved. It goes on to say, he has sworn by himself that every knee should bow, and every tongue swear. This is God's oath to save every bowed (subjection) knee to swear allegiance to Jesus. Paul stated, "For it is written, As I live, saith the Lord, every knee shall bow to me, and every tongue shall confess to God. So, then every one of us shall give an account of himself to God" (Rom 14:11–12).

95. Paul said, "That at the name of Jesus every knee should bow, of things in heaven, and things in earth, and things under the earth; And that every tongue should confess that Jesus Christ is Lord, to the glory of God the Father" (Philippians 2:10–11). The word "confess" means to be thankful, have gratitude or praise, which can only come from the heart. It is the same word used when Jesus said, "I thank thee O Father, Lord of heaven and earth, that thou hast hid these things from the wise and prudent . . ." (Luke 10:21). Everyone shall bow the knee in subjection and every tongue shall be thankful that Jesus is Lord!

This concludes this little book, be blessed for all things are out of God and shall return to Christ, The Original Matrix.

TDC

---

20. Hiett, *All Things New*, 38

Bibliography

Allin, Thomas. *Christ Triumphant, or Universalism Asserted as the Hope of the Gospel on the Authority of Reason, the Fathers, and Holy Scripture*, Canyon Country, CA, Concordant Concern.

Augustine. *The City of God,* Translated by Marcus Dods, Introduction by Kim Paffenroth, New York, Barnes & Noble, 2006.

Ballou, Hosea. *A Voice To Universalists*, Original Publisher—J.M. Usher, Boston, J. A. Gurley, Cincinnati, 1851, Classic Reprint Series, Forgotten Books, 2015.

Balthasar, Hans Urs von. *Explorations in Theology V, Man Is Created,* Translated by Adrian Walker, San Francisco, Ignatius, 2014.

———. *Dare We Hope "That All Men Be Saved"?, With a Short Discourse on Hell.* Translated by David Kipp and Lothar Krauth, San Francisco, Ignatius, 1988.

Campbell, Reginald John. *New Theology Sermons*, Williams and Norgate, London, Classic Reprint Series, Forgotten Books, 2015.

———. *The Song of Ages;* Scholar Select, New York, A.C. Armstrong & Son, 1905.

———. *The Life of the World to Come*, ISBN-9781446508800.

Cox, Samuel. *Salvator Mundi: Or, Is Christ the Saviour of All Men?,* Kegan Paul, Trench, Trubner & Co, Ltd, 1899.

Eby, J Preston. *The Saviour of the World Series—God All in All,* El Paso, TX, available online—www.kingdombiblestudies.org.

———. *The Seed In Every Man*, El Paso, TX, available online—www.kingdombible studies.org.

Fenton, Ferrar. *The Holy Bible in Modern English*, Merrimac MA, Destiny, 1966.

Gregory of Nyssa. *Nicene And Post-Nicene Fathers, Volume 5, Gregory of Nyssa: Dogmatic Series, Second Series, On The Making of Man,* Edited by Philip Schaff and Henry Wace, Hendrickson, 2012.

Hart, David Bentley. *That All shall be Saved, Heaven, Hell, and Universal Salvation,* Yale University Press, 2019.

Hiett, Peter. *All Things New*, Relentless Love, 2019 www.relentless-love.org

Ignatius. *Ante-Nicene Fathers, Volume 1, The Apostolic Fathers, Justin Martyr, Irenaeus; Epistle of Ignatius to the Magnesians,* 2012.

———. *Ante-Nicene Fathers, Volume 1 The Apostolic Fathers, Justin Martyr, Irenaeus; Epistle of Ignatius to the Trallians*, 2012.

Jukes, Andrew. *Restitution of All Things*, Canyon Country, CA, Concordant Concern, 1976.

MacDonald, George. *The Mirrors of the Lord in Unspoken Sermons, Series I, II, III Complete and Unabridged*, 2016.

———. *The New Name in Unspoken Sermons, Series I, II, III Complete and Unabridged*, 2016.

Murray, Richard. *Facebook posts*, 2020.

Origen. *On First Principles*, Foreword by John Cavadini, Introduction by Henri de Lubac, Notre Dame, Ave Maria Press, 2013.

———. *Homilies 1–14 on Ezekiel, Ancient Christian Writers* Translation by Thomas Scheck, New York, The Newman, 2010.

_____ *The Fathers of the Church—Homiles on Luke*, Translated by Joseph Lienhard, The Catholic University of American Press, 1996.

———. *The Fathers of the Church—Homiles on Genesis and Exodus*, Translated by Ronald Heine, The Catholic University of American Press, 1982.

Petrelli, Giuseppe, *Ecce Homo, Part Four—Behold The Man*, Binghamton, NY, Theophilus, 1962.

———. *Heavenward, Book III—Partakes of the Divine Nature*, Theophilus, 1953.

Prinzing, Ray. *Redemption . . . All In All*, Book by Prinzing, Boise ID.

Philo. *On Creation: The Works of Philo*, Translated by Charles Duke Yonge, Hendrickson, 1997.

Talbott, Thomas. *The Inescapable Love of God*, Eugene, OR, Wipf & Stock, 2014.

Thayer, Thomas Baldwin. *The Origin and History of the Doctrine of Endless Punishment; Scholar Select*, Universalist House, 1881.

———. *Theology of Universalism*, Classic Reprint Series, Forgotten Books 2012, Universalist House, 1891.

Winchester, Elhanan, *The Universal Restoration, Exhibited in Four Dialogues Between a Minister and His Friend*, Printed by Isaiah Whipple, 1803, Worchester, MA, Classic Reprint Series, Forgotten Books, 2015.

Zahnd, Brian. *Sinners in the Hands of a Loving God*, Foreword by William Paul Young, Colorado Springs, WaterBrook, 2017.

Printed in Great Britain
by Amazon

25195438R00046